Bertolt Brecht: Plays, Poetry and Prose

Edited by JOHN WILLETT *and* RALPH MANHEIM

Poems 1913–1956

Part Two 1929–1938

Bertolt Brecht Poems

Edited by JOHN WILLETT *and* RALPH MANHEIM
with the co-operation of Erich Fried

Part Two 1929–1938

LONDON
Eyre Methuen

Contents

THE TRANSLATORS

Edith Anderson · Anya Bostock · Derek Bowman ·
Eva Borneman · Lee Baxendall · Patrick Bridgwater ·
Alasdair Clayre · Robert Conard · Agnes Headlam-Morley ·
H. R. Hays · Michael Hamburger · Frank Jellinek ·
Frank Jones · Lesley Lendrum · Peter Levi ·
Christopher Middleton · Humphrey Milne ·
Michael Morley · Sammy McLean · Edith Roseveare ·
George Rapp · Naomi Replansky · Muriel Rukeyser ·
Stephen Spender · John Willett.

EDITORS' NOTE

For this paperback edition, the Brecht *Poems* have been split into three parts. The first contains our selection up to 1928 (the year of *The Threepenny Opera*); the second continues it up to 1938 (i.e. from the world economic crisis to the eve of the war); while the third contains the remainder, up to his death in 1956. Since the hardback volume from which all three derive is comprised in the general English-language edition of Brecht's work, those poems which occur elsewhere (i.e. primarily in the plays) are excluded. A fourth, companion paperback will contain a selection from them, and this will cover the whole time-span.

The pages of the present edition are numbered as in the hardback. However, it excludes the critial apparatus of that large volume; i.e. Brecht's own notes and comments on poetry, the note on 'The principal collections of Brecht's poems' (relating the poems to his sometimes unrealised plans for grouping and collecting them), and the fairly detailed notes on separate poems, which also give particulars of musical settings. The hardback volume also contains a much fuller introduction. Anybody seeking this information will have to consult the hardback volume. The paperbacks give the poems without explanation or comment.

The principles behind the selection, the general method of translation and the decision not to print the German originals are explained in the hardback introduction. The basic text followed is that of the 1967 German collected edition (major variations being shown in the notes). However, unlike the original editors we have tried to follow a chronological arrangement. The aim is to show the development of Brecht's poetry and its close relationship with the times through which he lived.

IV Poems of the Crisis Years
1929–1933

LATE LAMENTED FAME OF THE
GIANT CITY OF NEW YORK

1

Who is there still remembers
The fame of the giant city of New York
In the decade after the Great War?

2

What a melting pot was America in those days – celebrated
by poets!
God's own country!
Invoked just by the initials of its names:
U.S.A.
Like an unmistakable childhood friend whom everyone
knows.

3

This inexhaustible melting pot, so it was said
Received everything that fell into it and converted it
Within twice two weeks into something identifiable.
All races which landed on this zestful continent
Eagerly abandoned themselves and forgot their profoundest
characteristics
Like bad habits
In order to become
As quickly as possible like those who were so much at home
there.
And they received them with careless generosity as if they
were utterly different
(Differing only through the difference of their miserable
existences).
Like a good leaven they feared no
Mass of dough, however enormous: they knew
They would penetrate everything.
What fame! What a century!

4

Ah, those voices of their women coming from the sound-
    boxes!
Thus they sang (take good care of those records!) in the
    golden age.
Harmony of the evening waters at Miami!
Uncontainable gaiety of the generations driving fast over
    unending roads!
Mighty lamentations of women singing, faithfully mourning
Broad-chested men, but ever surrounded by
Broad-chested men!

5

They collected whole parks of rare human specimens
Fed them scientifically, bathed them and weighed them
So that their incomparable gestures might be perpetuated in
    photographs
For all who came after.

6

They raised up their gigantic buildings with incomparable
    waste
Of the best human material. Quite openly, before the whole
    world
They squeezed from their workers all that was in them
Fired rifles into the coal mines and threw their used-up bones
    and
Exhausted muscles on the streets with
Good-natured laughter.
But in sporting acknowledgement they reported
The same rough obstinacy in workers on strike
With homeric exaggeration.

7

Poverty was considered despicable there.
In the films of this blessed nation

Men down on their luck, on seeing the homes of the poor
      (which included pianos and leather couches)
Killed themselves out of hand.

8

What fame! What a century!
Oh we too demanded such broad-gauge overcoats of rough
      material
With the padded shoulders which make men so broad
That three of them fill the entire sidewalk.
We too sought to brake our gestures
Thrust our hands slowly into our pockets and work ourselves
      slowly
Out of the armchairs in which we had reclined (as for all
      eternity)
Like a whole State turning over
And we too stuffed our mouths full of chewing gum (Beech-
      nut)
Which was supposed eventually to push forward the jawbone
And sat with jaws ruminating as in endless greed.
To our faces too we wished to lend that feared impenetrability
Of the *poker-faced man* who propounded himself to his fellow-
      citizens
As an insoluble riddle.
We too perpetually smiled, as if before or after a good piece
      of business
Which is the proof of a well-ordered digestion.
We too liked to slap our companions (all of them future
      customers)
On arm and thigh and between the shoulder-blades
Testing how to get such fellows into our hands
By the same caressing or grabbing motions as for dogs.
So we imitated this renowned race of men who seemed
      destined
To rule the world by helping it to progress.

9

What confidence! What an inspiration!
Those machine rooms: the biggest in the world!
The car factories campaigned for an increase in the birthrate:
   they had started making cars (on hire purchase)
For the unborn. Whoever threw away
Practically unused clothing (but so
That it rotted at once, preferably in quicklime)
Was paid a bonus. Those bridges
Which linked flourishing land with flourishing land! Endless!
The longest in the world! Those skyscrapers –
The men who piled their stones so high
That they towered over all, anxiously watched from their
   summits the new buildings
Springing up from the ground, soon to overtower
Their own mammoth size.
(Some were beginning to fear that the growth of such cities
Could no longer be stopped, that they would have to finish
   their days
With twenty storeys of other cities above them
And would be stacked in coffins which would be buried
One on top of the other.)

10

But apart from that: what confidence! Even the dead
Were made up and given a cosy smile
(These are characteristics I am setting down from memory;
   others
I have forgotten) for not even those who had got away
Were allowed to be without hope.

11

What people they were! Their boxers the strongest!
Their inventors the most practical! Their trains the fastest!
And also the most crowded!
And it all looked like lasting a thousand years

For the people of the city of New York put it about them-
      selves:
That their city was built on the rock and hence
Indestructible.

12

Truly their whole system of communal life was beyond com-
      pare.
What fame! What a century!

13

Admittedly that century lasted
A bare eight years.

14

For one day there ran through the world the rumour of
      strange collapses
On a famous continent, and its banknotes, hoarded only
      yesterday
Were rejected in disgust like rotten stinking fish.

15

Today, when the word has gone round
That these people are bankrupt
We on the other continents (which are indeed bankrupt as
      well)
See many things differently and, so we think, more clearly.

16

What of the skyscrapers?
We observe them more coolly.
What contemptible hovels skyscrapers are when they no
      longer yield rents!
Rising so high, full of poverty? Touching the clouds, full of
      debt?
What of the railroad trains?

In the railroad trains, which resemble hotels on wheels, they
    say
Often nobody lives.
He travels nowhere
With incomparable rapidity.
What of the bridges? The longest in the world, they now link
Scrapheap with scrapheap.
And what of the people?

17

They still make up, we hear, but now
It's to grab a job. Twenty-two year old girls
Sniff cocaine now before setting out
To capture a place at a typewriter.
Desperate parents inject poison into their daughters' thighs
To make them look red hot.

18

Gramophone records are still sold, not many of course
But what do they tell us, these cows who have not learned
To sing? What
Is the sense of these songs? What have they really
Been singing to us all these years long?
Why do we now dislike these once celebrated voices?
Why
Do these photos of cities no longer make the slightest impres-
    sion on us?
Because word has gone round
That these people are bankrupt.

19

For their machines, it is said, lie in huge heaps (the biggest
    in the world)
And rust
Like the machines of the Old World (in smaller heaps).

20

World championships are still contested before a few specta-
tors who have absent-mindedly stayed in their places:
Each time the strongest competitor
Stands no chance against the mysterious law
That drives people away from shops stocked to bursting.

21

Clutching their smile (but nothing else now) the retired world
champions
Stand in the way of the last few streetcars left running.
Three of these broad-gauge fellows fill the sidewalk, but
What will fill *them* before nightfall?
The padding warms only the shoulders of those who in inter-
minable columns
Hurry day and night through the empty canyons of lifeless
stonepiles.
Their gestures are slow, like those of hungry and enfeebled
beasts.
Like a whole State turning over
They work themselves slowly out of the gutters in which they
seem to be lying as for all eternity.
Their confidence, it is said
Is still there; it is based on the hope that
Tomorrow the rain will fall upwards.

22

But some, we hear, can still find jobs: in those places
Where whole waggon-loads of wheat are being shovelled into
the ocean
Called pacific.
And those who spend their nights on benches are, we hear,
apt to
Think quite impermissible thoughts as they see
Those empty skyscrapers before dropping off to sleep.

23

What a bankruptcy! How
Great a fame has departed! What a discovery:
That their system of communal life displays
The same miserable flaw as that of
More modest people.

THE CARPET WEAVERS OF
KUYAN-BULAK HONOUR LENIN

1

Often and copiously honour has been done
To Comrade Lenin. There are busts and statues.
Cities are called after him, and children.
Speeches are made in many languages
There are meetings and demonstrations
From Shanghai to Chicago in Lenin's honour.
But this is how he was honoured by
The carpet weavers of Kuyan-Bulak
A little township in southern Turkestan.

Every evening there twenty carpet weavers
Shaking with fever rise from their primitive looms.
Fever is rife: the railway station
Is full of the hum of mosquitoes, a thick cloud
That rises from the swamp behind the old camels' graveyard.
But the railway train which
Every two weeks brings water and smoke, brings
The news also one day
That the day approaches for honouring Comrade Lenin.
And the people of Kuyan-Bulak
Carpet weavers, poor people
Decide that in their township too Comrade Lenin's
Plaster bust shall be put up.
Then, as the collection is made for the bust
They all stand

Shaking with fever and offer
Their hard-earned kopeks with trembling hands.
And the Red Army man Stepa Gamalev, who
Carefully counts and minutely watches
Sees how ready they are to honour Lenin, and he is glad
But he also sees their unsteady hands
And he suddenly proposes
That the money for the bust be used to buy petroleum
To be poured on the swamp behind the camels' graveyard
Where the mosquitoes breed that carry
The fever germ.
And so to fight the fever at Kuyan-Bulak, thus
Honouring the dead but
Never to be forgotten
Comrade Lenin.

They resolved to do this. On the day of the ceremony they
        carried
Their dented buckets filled with black petroleum
One after the other
And poured it over the swamp.

So they helped themselves by honouring Lenin, and
Honoured him by helping themselves, and thus
Had understood him well.

2
We have heard how the people of Kuyan-Bulak
Honoured Lenin. When in the evening
The petroleum had been bought and poured on the swamp
A man rose at the meeting, demanding
That a plaque be affixed on the railway station
Recording these events and containing
Precise details too of their altered plan, the exchange of
The bust for Lenin for a barrel of fever-destroying oil.
And all this in honour of Lenin.
And they did this as well
And put up the plaque.

EPITAPH, 1919

Red Rosa now has vanished too.
Where she lies is hid from view.
She told the poor what life is about
And so the rich have rubbed her out.

ON EVERYDAY THEATRE

You artists who perform plays
In great houses under electric suns
Before the hushed crowd, pay a visit some time
To that theatre whose setting is the street.
The everyday, thousandfold, fameless
But vivid, earthy theatre fed by the daily human contact
Which takes place in the street.
Here the woman from next door imitates the landlord:
Demonstrating his flood of talk she makes it clear
How he tried to turn the conversation
From the burst water pipe. In the parks at night
Young fellows show giggling girls
The way they resist, and in resisting
Slyly flaunt their breasts. A drunk
Gives us the preacher at his sermon, referring the poor
To the rich pastures of paradise. How useful
Such theatre is though, serious and funny
And how dignified! They do not, like parrot or ape
Imitate just for the sake of imitation, unconcerned
What they imitate, just to show that they
Can imitate; no, they
Have a point to put across. You
Great artists, masterly imitators, in this regard
Do not fall short of them! Do not become too remote
However much you perfect your art
From that theatre of daily life
Whose setting is the street.

Take that man on the corner: he is showing how
An accident took place. This very moment
He is delivering the driver to the verdict of the crowd. The
        way he
Sat behind the steering wheel, and now
He imitates the man who was run over, apparently
An old man. Of both he gives
Only so much as to make the accident intelligible, and yet
Enough to make you see them. But he shows neither
As if the accident had been unavoidable. The accident
Becomes in this way intelligible, yet not intelligible, for both
        of them
Could have moved quite otherwise; now he is showing what
They might have done so that no accident
Would have occurred. There is no superstition
About this eyewitness, he
Shows mortals as victims not of the stars, but
Only of their errors.

Note also
His earnestness and the accuracy of his imitation. He
Knows that much depends on his exactness: whether the
        innocent man
Escapes ruin, whether the injured man
Is compensated. Watch him
Repeat now what he did just before. Hesitantly
Calling on his memory for help, uncertain
Whether his demonstration is good, interrupting himself
And asking someone else to
Correct him on a detail. This
Observe with reverence!
And with surprise
Observe, if you will, one thing: that this imitator
Never loses himself in his imitation. He never entirely
Transforms himself into the man he is imitating. He always
Remains the demonstrator, the one not involved. The man
Did not open his heart to him, he

Does not share his feelings
Or his opinions. He knows hardly anything
About him. In his imitation
No third thing rises out of him and the other
Somehow consisting of both, in which supposedly
One heart beats and
One brain thinks. Himself all there
The demonstrator stands and gives us
The stranger next door.

The mysterious transformation
That allegedly goes on in your theatres
Between dressing room and stage – an actor
Leaves the dressing room, a king
Appears on the stage: that magic
Which I have often seen reduce the stagehands, beerbottles in
    hand
To laughter –
Does not occur here.
Our demonstrator at the street corner
Is no sleepwalker who must not be addressed. He is
No high priest holding divine service. At any moment
You can interrupt him; he will answer you
Quite calmly and when you have spoken with him
Go on with his performance.

But you, do not say: that man
Is not an artist. By setting up such a barrier
Between yourselves and the world, you simply
Expel yourselves from the world. If you thought him
No artist he might think you
Not human, and that
Would be a worse reproach. Say rather:
He is an artist because he is human. We
May do what he does more perfectly and
Be honoured for it, but what we do
Is something universal, human, something hourly

Practised in the busy street, almost
As much a part of life as eating and breathing.

Thus your playacting
Harks back to practical matters. Our masks, you should say
Are nothing special insofar as they are only masks:
There the scarf peddler
Puts on a derby like a masher's
Hooks a cane over his arm, even pastes a moustache
Under his nose and struts a step or two
Behind his stand, thus
Pointing out what wonders
Men can work with scarves, moustaches and hats. And our
        verses, you should say
In themselves are not extraordinary – the newsboys
Shout the headlines in cadences, thereby
Intensifying the effect and making their frequent repetition
Easier. We
Speak other men's lines, but lovers
And salesmen also learn other men's lines, and how often
All of you quote sayings! In short
Mask, verse and quotation are common, but uncommon
The grandly conceived mask, the beautifully spoken verse
And apt quotation.

But to make matters clear: even if you improved upon
What the man at the corner did, you would be doing less
Than him if you
Made your theatre less meaningful – with lesser provocation
Less intense in its effect on the audience – and
Less useful.

ADVICE TO THE ACTRESS C.N.

Refresh yourself, sister
With the water from the copper bowl with bits of ice in it –

Open your eyes under water, wash them –
Dry yourself with the rough towel and cast
A glance at a book you love.
In this way begin
A lovely and useful day.

SONNET ON A NEW EDITION OF FRANÇOIS
VILLON

Once more the fading letters come up clear
In this new version of his Testament
Where he doles out his lumps of excrement –
Will all who want a piece please answer 'Here!'?

Where is the snot you spat as he walked past?
Where is the man you told to stuff himself?
His verse has lasted longest on the shelf
But how much longer is it going to last?

Here, for the price of fifty cigarettes
You buy another chance to read it through
(And thus to find out what he thought of you . . .)

It's sour but cheap; you pay three marks for it
And what a lucky dip the buyer gets!
I for my own part fished out quite a bit . . .

HIS END

So that a moon might touch his death with glamour
He left the town before the end was near
And rapidly, where silence confronts clamour
Reached the poor line they'd fixed as their frontier.

There between three corrugated sheds
And a fir tree that somehow had been left upright

He chewed his last mouthfuls to shreds
And passed one last dreamless night.

Next morning was spent on all sorts of things.
By noon it was still not warm. A northerly breeze blew in.
Clouds, breaking up over the woods around five o'clock
Never got to him.

Towards midnight three continents went under
Towards dawn America crumbled away
So that when he died it was as if none of it had ever been
Neither what he saw, nor what he did not see.

.

A BED FOR THE NIGHT

I hear that in New York
At the corner of 26th Street and Broadway
A man stands every evening during the winter months
And gets beds for the homeless there
By appealing to passers-by

It won't change the world
It won't improve relations among men
It will not shorten the age of exploitation
But a few men have a bed for the night
For a night the wind is kept from them
The snow meant for them falls on the roadway.

Don't put down the book on reading this, man.

A few people have a bed for the night
For a night the wind is kept from them
The snow meant for them falls on the roadway
But it won't change the world
It won't improve relations among men
It will not shorten the age of exploitation.

ARTICLE ONE OF THE WEIMAR CONSTITUTION

1

From the People proceeds the power of the State.
– But where does it proceed to?
Yes, where is it proceeding to?
There's some place it's proceeding to.
The policeman proceeds through the station gate.
– But where does he proceed to?
etc.

2

Look, there's the whole lot on the march.
– But where are they marching to?
Yes, where are they marching to?
There's some place they are marching to.
They wheel through the gate and under the arch.
– But where are they wheeling to?
etc.

3

The power of the State turns right about.
Something is in the air.
– What can be in the air?
There's something in the air.
The power of the State gives a piercing shout
And yells: Get moving there!
– But moving why and where?
It yells: Get moving there!

4

There's something standing in a crowd
Something which queries that.
Why should it query that?
What cheek to query that!
The State just shoots – for that's allowed –
And something falls down flat.

What was it fell down flat?
What made it fall like that?

5
The power of the State sees something spill.
Something lies in the shit.
What's lying in the shit?
Something's lying in the shit.
There's something lying deadly still
– The People, why, that's it!
Can that really be it?
Yes, that is really it.

THE SPRING

1
Springtime is coming.
The play of the sexes renews itself
That's when the lovers start to come together.
One gentle caress from the hand of her loved one
Has the girl's breast starting to tingle.
Her least glance will overwhelm him.

2
A new-found light
Reveals the countryside to lovers in springtime.
At a great height the first
Flocks of birds are sighted.
The air's turning warm.
The days are getting long and the
Fields stay light a long time.

3
Boundless is the growth of all trees and all grasses
In springtime.
Incessantly fruitful

Is the land, are the meadows, the forest.
And the earth gives birth to the new
Heedless of caution.

BALLAD OF THE DROP IN THE OCEAN

1

The summer has arrived, and the summer sky
Shines on you too.
The water is warm, and in the warm water
You too lie.
On the green meadows you have
Pitched your tents. The roads
Heard your singing. The forest
Welcomes you. So
    You're no longer poor? There's more in the pot?
    You're being cared for? Content with your lot?
    So things are looking up, then? They're not:
    It's a drop in the ocean, that's what.

2

The forest has welcomed men with no homes. The lovely sky
Is shining on men with no hope. Those living in summer tents
Have no other shelter. Those lying in the warm water
Have not eaten. Those
Tramping the roads were simply carrying on
Their incessant search for work.
    You're still as poor. There's no more in the pot.
    You're not being cared for. You can't accept your lot.
    Are things looking up, then? No, they're not:
    It's a drop in the ocean, that's what.

3

Will you be content with nothing but the shining sky?
Will the warm water never release you again?

Will the forest hold on to you?
Are you being fobbed off? Are you being consoled?
The world is waiting for you to put your demands
It needs your discontent, your suggestions.
The world is looking to you with its last shred of hope.
  It's time you firmly said you will not
  Accept the drop, but must have the whole lot.

SOLIDARITY SONG

Peoples of the world, together
Join to serve the common cause!
So it feeds us all for ever
See to it that it's now yours.
  Forward, without forgetting
  Where our strength can be seen now to be!
  When starving or when eating
  Forward, not forgetting
  Our solidarity!

Black or white or brown or yellow
Leave your old disputes behind.
Once start talking with your fellow
Men, you'll soon be of one mind.
  Forward, without forgetting
  Where our strength can be seen now to be!
  When starving or when eating
  Forward, not forgetting
  Our solidarity!

If we want to make this certain
We'll need you and your support.
It's yourselves you'll be deserting
If you rat on your own sort.

Forward, without forgetting
Where our strength can be seen now to be!
When starving or when eating
Forward, not forgetting
Our solidarity!

All the gang of those who rule us
Hope our quarrels never stop
Helping them to split and fool us
So they can remain on top.
Forward, without forgetting
Where our strength can be seen now to be!
When starving or when eating
Forward, not forgetting
Our solidarity!

Workers of the world, uniting
That's the way to lose your chains.
Mighty regiments now are fighting
That no tyranny remains!
Forward, without forgetting
Till the concrete question is hurled
When starving or when eating:
Whose tomorrow is tomorrow?
And whose world is the world?

THE BALLAD OF PARAGRAPH 218

Please, doctor. I've missed my monthly . . .
Why, this is simply great.
If I may put it bluntly
You're raising our birthrate.
Please, doctor, now we're homeless . . .
But you'll have a bed somewhere
So best put your feet up, moan less
And force yourself to grin and bear.

You'll make a simply splendid little mummy
Producing cannon-fodder from your tummy
That's what your body's for, and you know it, what's more
And it's laid down by law
And now get this straight:
You'll soon be a mother, just wait.

But, doctor, no job or dwelling:
My man would find kids the last straw . . .
No, rather a new compelling
Objective to work for.
But, doctor . . . Really, Frau Griebel
I ask myself what this means
You see, our State needs people
To operate our machines.
You'll make a simply splendid little mummy
Producing factory fodder from your tummy
That's what your body's for, and you know it, what's more
And it's laid down by law
And now get this straight:
You'll soon be a mother, just wait.

But, doctor, there's such unemployment . . .
I can't follow what you say.
You're all out for enjoyment
Then grumble at having to pay.
If we make a prohibition
You bet we've a purpose in mind.
Better recognise your condition
And once you've agreed to put yourselves in our hands, you'll
        find
You're a simply splendid little mummy
Producing cannon fodder from your tummy
That's what your body's for, and you know it, what's more
And it's laid down by law
And now get this straight:
You'll soon be a mother, just wait.

LULLABIES

I

When I gave you birth that day your brothers were crying
For soup, and we hadn't any.
When I gave you birth you found the world without much
     light
Because we couldn't pay the gas-man his money.

When I was carrying you inside me
I often talked about you with your Dad
But we couldn't pay for any visits from the doctor;
The food cost all we had.

When I conceived you we'd given up all hope
Of getting work or bread.
Only in Karl Marx and Lenin could we workers
See a chance of life ahead.

II

When I carried you in my body
There was no hope anywhere
And I often said: it's an evil world
That's waiting for the one I bear.

And I decided I'd make certain
That he wouldn't go astray.
The one I carry must help to see
It's a better world one day.

And I said, as I passed the mountains
Of fenced-in coal: it's all right.
The one I'm bearing will see that this coal
Warms him and gives him light.

And when I saw loaves in windows
That the hungry passed, I said:
The one I'm carrying in my body
Will see that he eats this bread.

And they came and took his father
And they killed him in the war.
I said: the one I'm bearing will see
They don't take any more.

As I carried you in my body
I would often softly say:
You inside my body
Nothing must block your way.

III

I gave you birth, when birth was
A dangerous thing to give
When it was brave to conceive you
And a battle to let you live.

Old Blücher and all his captains
Would have been lost, my son
Where a couple of baby's napkins
Are victories to be won.

Yes, bread and milk are victories
And heat in the room a fight.
To get you up to manhood
I must struggle day and night.

For a scrap of bread to give you
Means manning picket ranks
And conquering mighty generals
And charging guns and tanks.

Yet when I've got you to manhood
I'll have gathered one more in
To join us in the struggle
And fight until we win.

IV
My son, whatever you do or try to do
There's a line of them waiting with truncheons steady
For there's only one bit of space on this earth for you:
The rubbish dump, and it's occupied already.

My son, you must listen to your mother when she tells you
It'll be worse than the plague, the life you've got in store.
But don't think I brought you into the world so painfully
To lie down under it and meekly ask for more.

What you don't have, don't ever abandon.
What they don't give you, get yourself and keep.
I, your mother, haven't borne and fed you
To see you crawl one night under a railway arch to sleep.

I don't say you're made of anything special;
I can't give you money, or kneel by you and pray;
But I hope – and I've nothing but you to build on –
You won't watch labour exchanges gradually stamp your life
        away.

When in the night I lie and stare unsleeping
Often I turn and reach out for your hand.
How can I make you see through their lying?
I know you've been numbered for wars they've already
        planned.

Your mother, my son, has never pretended
You're the special son of someone special's daughter;
But neither did she bring you up with so much hardship
To hang on the barbed wire one day crying for water.

And so, my son, stay close to your own people
So your power, like the dust, will spread to every place.
You, my son, and I and all our people
Must stand together till there are no longer two unequal
Classes to divide the entire human race.

SONG OF THE S.A. MAN

My hunger made me fall asleep
With a belly ache.
Then I heard voices crying
Hey, Germany awake!

Then I saw crowds of men marching:
To the Third Reich, I heard them say.
I thought as I'd nothing to live for
I might as well march their way.

And as I marched, there marched beside me
The fattest of that crew
And when I shouted 'We want bread and work'
The fat man shouted too.

The chief of staff wore boots
My feet meanwhile were wet
But both of us were marching
Wholeheartedly in step.

I thought that the left road led forward
He told me that I was wrong.
I went the way that he ordered
And blindly tagged along.

And those who were weak from hunger
Kept marching, pale and taut
Together with the well-fed
To some Third Reich of a sort.

They told me which enemy to shoot at
So I took their gun and aimed
And, when I had shot, saw my brother
Was the enemy they had named.

Now I know: over there stands my brother
It's hunger that makes us one
While I march with the enemy
My brother's and my own.

So now my brother is dying
By my own hand he fell
Yet I know that if he's defeated
I shall be lost as well.

OF ALL THE WORKS OF MAN

Of all the works of man I like best
Those which have been used.
The copper pots with their dents and flattened edges
The knives and forks whose wooden handles
Have been worn away by many hands: such forms
Seemed to me the noblest. So too the flagstones round old
     houses
Trodden by many feet, ground down
And with tufts of grass growing between them: these
Are happy works.

Absorbed into the service of the many
Frequently altered, they improve their shape, grow precious
Because so often appreciated.
Even broken pieces of sculpture
With their hands lopped off, are dear to me. They too
Were alive for me. They were dropped, yet they were also
     carried.
They were knocked down, yet they never stood too high.

Half ruined buildings once again take on
The look of buildings waiting to be finished
Generously planned: their fine proportions
Can already be guessed at, but they still
Need our understanding. At the same time
They have already served, indeed have already been over-
      come. All this
Delights me.

ABOUT THE WAY TO CONSTRUCT ENDURING WORKS

I
1
How long
Do works endure? As long
As they are not completed.
Since as long as they demand effort
They do not decay.

Inviting further work
Repaying participation
Their being lasts as long as
They invite and reward.

Useful works
Require people
Artistic works
Have room for art
Wise works
Require wisdom
Those devised for completeness
Show gaps
The long-lasting
Are always about to crumble
Those planned on a really big scale

Are unfinished.
Still imperfect
Like a wall awaiting the ivy
(It was once unfinished
Long ago, before the ivy came; bare).

Still short-lived
Like a machine that is used
But is not good enough
But gives promise of a better model
Work for endurance must
Be built like
A machine full of shortcomings.

2
So too the games we invent
Are unfinished, we hope;
And the things we use in playing
What are they without the dentings from
Many fingers, those places, seemingly damaged
Which produce nobility of form;
And the words too whose
Meaning often changed
With change of users.

3
Never go forward without going
Back first to check the direction.
Those who ask questions are those
Whom you will answer, but
Those who will listen to you are
Those who then ask you.

Who will speak?
He who has not spoken.
Who will enter?
He who has not yet entered.

Those whose position seems insignificant
When one looks at them
Are
The powerful ones of tomorrow
Those who have need of you
Shall have the power.

Who gives works duration?
Those who'll be alive then.
Whom to choose as builders?
Those still unborn.

Do not ask what they will be like. But
Determine it.

II

If something is to be said which will not be understood at
        once
If advice is given which takes long to carry out
If man's infirmity is feared, or
The perseverance of enemies, all-shattering cataclysms
Then works must be given long duration.

III

The desire to make works of long duration
Is not always to be welcomed.

He who addresses himself to the unborn
Often does nothing towards their birth.
He does not fight yet wishes to win.
He sees no enemy
But oblivion.

Why should every wind endure for ever?
A good expression is worth noting

So long as the occasion can recur
For which it was good.
Certain experiences handed on in perfect form
Enrich mankind
But richness can become too much.
Not only the experiences
But their recollection too ages one.

Therefore the desire to make works of long duration is
Not always to be welcomed.

BALLAD ON APPROVING OF THE WORLD

1

I'm not unjust, but not courageous either:
They pointed out their world to me today
I only saw the bloody pointing finger
And quickly said I liked the world that way.

2

I stood facing their world, beneath their truncheons
And spent the whole day judging what I saw.
Saw butchers who seemed suited to their functions
When I was asked 'D'you like it?' I said 'Sure'.

3

And from that moment my proclaimed opinion
Was: better cowardly than in one's grave.
To keep from falling under their dominion
I kept approving what one can't approve.

4

I saw the crops, and Junkers profiteering.
With hollow cheeks the people doffed their caps.
I tried the wheat, and told all within hearing:
It's excellent – a trifle dear, perhaps.

5

Then the industrialists: such crippling losses
They can't find work for more than one in three
I told the other two: Best ask the bosses
I'm ignorant about economy.

6

I saw their troops preferring guns to butter
And planning whom to murder and to rob.
I called out as I stepped down in the gutter:
Credit where credit's due, they know their job!

7

The deputies who tell the starving voters
That they will make things better before long –
I call them brilliant speakers, say they didn't
Intend to lie, they merely got it wrong.

8

Saw civil servants, green with mildew, keeping
Their huge manure contraption on the move
So badly paid for bullying and creeping
I really hope their salaries improve.

9

The police, of course, must not think they're abandoned.
I give them, and the magistrate beside
A dainty towel to wipe their bloody hands on
So they may know that they're not being denied.

10

The judge who sees that property's protected
Letting his robes conceal his blood-smeared shoe
I can't insult him, or I'll be ejected
But, if I don't I'll know not what I do.

11

I say: these gentlemen can't be persuaded
For any sum, at any time of day
To carry out the law and enforce justice:
That's incorruptibility, would you not say?

12

Close by, I see some thugs maltreating
The wives and children, and the old and lame
And then I see the truncheons they are wielding.
So these aren't thugs: they have another name.

13

The police, who battle with the underfed
To stop us sharing their distressing lot
Have far too much to do. If they'll protect me
From burglary, they can have all I've got.

14

Well, now I've proved to you that I am harmless
I hope that you will look the other way
While I confess I'm wholly for those people
Of whom the press has nothing good to say –

15

The journalists. They use the victims' entrails
To scrawl the words: The murderers didn't do it.
I pass you on the freshly printed details
And say: How well they write; you should glance through it.

16

The author has us read his Magic Mountain
What he wrote there (for money) was well thought up.
What he suppressed (for free): that was the real thing.
I say that man(n) is blind; he's not been bought up.

17

That tradesman there, assuring all and sundry
It's not my fish but I who really smell
Won't eat bad fish himself. I'll cultivate him
Hoping that he may find me fit to sell.

18

That man who's almost eaten up by pustules
And buys a girl with cash he shouldn't have –
I press his hand with warmth, but also caution
And say, Bless you for keeping her alive.

19

The doctors who chuck back their poorer patients
Like anglers throwing back a too small fish
I can't avoid, and lay my sickly body
Upon their couch to do with as they wish.

20

The engineers who thought up mass production
To milk the workers of their energy –
I praise them for their technical perfection.
It's such sheer mastery it makes me cry.

21

I saw teachers, those poor flagellators
Imposing their own image on the young.
That's what they get salaries from the state for.
It's that or starve. You'd blame them? Hold your tongue!

22

Children I see in early adolescence
Who look like six, and speak like seventy.
That's life, I say. To the unspoken question
Why should it be? I say: Ah, there you have me.

23

And the professors, whose imposing phrases
Condone the thugs by whom they are directed –
Crime wrapped in talk of economic crises –
No one can say they're worse than I expected.

24

And scholarship which, adding to our knowledge
Also turns out to add to our distress
Deserves to be as honoured as religion
Which adds to ignorance and is not honoured less.

25

Enough of that. The priests are quite close to me.
Through war and butchery they guard the flame
Of faith in love and charity above us:
That's one thing to be set beside their name.

26

I saw a world which worships God and profits
Heard hunger shout: Give something! Saw a pair
Of pudgy fingers pointing up to heaven.
Said: There you are, there must be something there.

27

My friend George Grosz's men with heads like bullets –
You know them from his drawings – are, it seems
About to slit the human race's gullets.
I give my full approval to their schemes.

28

I saw the murderers and the victims also
And, lacking courage but not sympathy
Observed the murderers picking out their victims
And shouted: I approve wholeheartedly!

29

I see them coming, see the butchers marching
Would like to bawl out 'Stop!', but as meanwhile
I know their agents are beside me watching
I hear my own voice bawling at them 'Heil!'

30

Since poverty and baseness leave me cold
My pen falls silent; times are on the move
Yet all that's dirty in your dirty world
Includes, I know, the fact that I approve.

IN SMOLNY DURING THE SUMMER OF 1917 THE BOLSHEVIKS DISCOVERED WHERE THE PEOPLE WERE REPRESENTED – IN THE KITCHEN

When the February Revolution was over and the movement
        of the masses
Came to a halt
The war was not yet ended. The peasants were landless
The workers in the factories oppressed and starving.
But the soviets were elected by all and represented a few.
Seeing that everything thus remained as it was and nothing
        altered
The Bolsheviks went about in the soviets like criminals
For they kept demanding that the guns
Should be turned against the proletariat's real enemy:
The rulers.
So they were regarded as traitors and treated as counter-
        revolutionaries
Representatives of a mob of bandits. Their leader Lenin
Dubbed spy and hireling, hid in a barn.
Whichever way they looked
People looked away, silence met them.
Under other flags they saw the masses marching.

A great figure was cut by the bourgeois generals and
    merchants
Till the Bolshevik cause appeared lost.
During this time they went on working as usual
Paying no attention to the hullabaloo and little to the plain
    defection
Of those they were fighting for. Rather, they
Forever continued
Campaigning with ever fresh efforts
For the cause of the undermost.
This is the kind of thing that, by their own account, they
    seem to have taken note of:
In the Smolny canteen they observed
That when the food, cabbage soup and tea, was being dished
    out
The Executive Committee's waiter, a soldier, gave the
    Bolsheviks
Hotter tea and thicker-spread sandwiches
Than all the others: he handed it to them
Averting his eyes. In this way they realised, here
They had a sympathiser who was concealing the fact
From his superiors, and similarly
The entire junior personnel of Smolny
Guards, messengers and sentries, could be seen to be swinging
    towards them.
When they saw this they said:
'That's half the battle'.
In short, the slightest move on such people's part
Utterance or look, but likewise silence and the averted gaze
Struck them as important. And to be treated as
Friends by these people – that was their main objective.

THE INTERNATIONALE

Comrades report:
In the foothills of the Pamir

We met a woman in charge of a small cocoon farm
Who has convulsions whenever she hears the
Internationale. She told her story:
In the civil war her husband was
The leader of a band of partisans. Gravely wounded
Lying in their hut, he was betrayed. Taking him captive
The White Guards cried: You won't be singing your
Internationale much longer! And before his eyes
They seized his wife and raped her on the bed.
Then the man began to sing.
And he sang the Internationale
Even when they shot his youngest child
And he ceased singing
When they took and shot his son
And he ceased living. Since that day
The woman says, she has had convulsions
When she hears the Internationale.
And, she tells us, it has been very hard
To find a place to work in any of the Soviet republics
Where one doesn't hear the song sung
For from Moscow to the Pamir
These days you can't escape the sound of
The Internationale. But it is heard less often
In the Pamir.
And we continued talking of her work.
She told us: So far the district
Has only half fulfilled the Plan.
But her locality is already quite transformed
Unrecognisable, it yet grows daily more familiar
A new crowd of people is providing
New work, new leisure
And by next year it is likely
The Plan will be exceeded
And once this happens, then they'll build
A factory here: once that is built
Well, she said, on that day I shall
Sing the Internationale.

AWAITING THE SECOND FIVE-YEAR PLAN

At this time of growing confusion all over our planet
We await the second plan
Of the first communist society.

This plan provides not for
An eternally valid ordering of social rank
Or a brilliant way of organising famine
Or the good discipline of the exploited
But for the full satisfaction of everybody's needs
According to intelligible principles.

It is not from the strength of a race
Not from the inspiration of a Führer
Not from special devices, superhuman miracles
But from a simple plan
Realisable by any people of any race
Based on plain considerations such as can occur to anyone
Who is neither an exploiter nor an oppressor
That we await everything.

SONG OF THE FLOCKS OF STARLINGS

1
We set out in the month of October
In the province of Suiyan
We flew fast in a southerly direction straight
Through four provinces, taking five days.
   Fly faster, the plains are waiting
   The cold increases and
   There it is warm.

2
We set out, eight thousand of us
From the province of Suiyan

We grew by thousands each day, the farther we came
Through four provinces, taking five days.
  Fly faster, the plains are waiting
  The cold increases and
  There it is warm.

3
Now we are flying over the plain
In the province of Hunan
We see great nets beneath us and know
Where we have flown to, taking five days:
  The plains have waited
  The warmth increases and
  Our death is certain.

WHEN THE FASCISTS KEPT GETTING STRONGER

When the Fascists kept getting stronger in Germany
And even workers were joining them in growing masses
We said to ourselves: We fought the wrong way.
All through our red Berlin the Nazis strutted, in fours and
      fives
In their new uniforms, murdering
Our comrades.
But among the dead were people from the Reichsbanner as
      well as people of ours
So we said to the comrades of the SPD:
Are we to stand by while they murder our comrades?
Fight alongside us in the Anti-Fascist Front!
This is the answer we got:
We would perhaps fight alongside you, but our leaders
Keep advising us not to match white terror with red terror.
Every day, we said, our paper warns us against individual
      acts of terror
But it also warns us every day: we can only win through with
A united Red Front.

Comrades, do get it into your heads, this 'lesser evil' which
Year after year has been used to keep you completely out of
      the fight
Will very soon mean having to stomach the Nazis.
But in the factories and all the dole queues
We saw the workers ready to fight.
In Berlin's eastern districts Social Democrats called
'Red Front!' in greeting, and even wore the badge
Of the anti-fascist movement. The pubs
Were full to bursting on discussion nights
And from that moment no Nazi
Dared walk the streets on his own
For the streets at least remain ours
Even if the houses are theirs.

BALLAD OF THE BRANCHES AND THE TRUNK

1

And they suddenly all descended in drab brown cotton shirts
All the bread and dripping disappeared
And they gobbled up all they could find there, spouting their
      indecent words
Till the table was cleared.
Let's stick around and play here, that's what they said
We've found a place to stay here, that's what they said
For at least one thousand years.
   Right. So much for the branches.
   Meanwhile the trunk keeps still.
   The guests all bawl for their lunches
   Till the landlord brings the bill.

2

And they found themselves good positions, and they ordered
      brand-new desks
And they looked around with pride.
They never worked out the expenses and they didn't reckon
      the risks

That's where they were planning to reside.
Let's stick around and play here, that's what they said
We've found a place to stay here, that's what they said
As they put their boots outside.
  Right. So much for the branches.
  Meanwhile the trunk keeps still.
  The guests all bawl for their lunches
  Till the landlord brings the bill.

3

And they love to loose off revolvers at the sight of a decent
      face
And they always go around in pairs.
And they go and fish out three marks only from their precious
      hideaway place
Glad to shrug off their cares.
We'll never need to pay here, that's what they said
Let's stick around and play here, that's what they said
Till we're all millionaires.
  Right. So much for the branches.
  Meanwhile the trunk keeps still.
  The guests all bawl for their lunches
  Till the landlord brings the bill.

4

And their housepainter painted over all the gaping cracks in
      the walls
And they made us all move as one.
And if you believe their story we'd all be the dearest of pals:
They thought we'd jump to their gun.
We only need to stay here, that's what they said
We're bound to get our way here, that's what they said
Now the Third Reich has begun.
  Right. So much for the branches.
  Meanwhile the trunk keeps still.
  The guests all bawl for their lunches
  Till the landlord brings the bill.

HITLER CHORALE I
(Tune: Now thank we all our God.)

1

Now thank we all our God
For sending Hitler to us;
From Germany's fair land
To clear away the rubbish
We've done with the old ways
The new paint's spick and span
So thank we all our God
Who sent us such a man.

2

The house was far too old
It let in wind and weather.
We'd soon have had to build
A new one altogether.
We thought the house would fall
Its rottenness was plain
But Hitler paints it all
So it stands firm again.

3

There's hunger everywhere
And no bread in the larder
We had no clothes to wear
When first we saw our Leader.
If we were still more tired
And hungrier today
He'd feed the multitude
With a single truss of hay.

4

The rich possess the bread.
The poor are almost fainting.
O merciful Godhead
We sorely need repainting

Lest the poor man should think
His hunger pangs to still
And fall upon the rich
At last to eat his fill.

5

But when our Hitler comes
He will redecorate us
Let each stay rich or poor
According to his status.
He'll see that class remains
But never leads to hate.
He'll make sure that it rains
But nobody gets wet.

6

He'll make the vinegar sweet
And make the sugar sour
From cracks in the concrete
He'll make a lofty tower.
He'll paint the filth and rot
Until it's spick and span
So thank we all our God
For sending us this man.

HITLER CHORALE III
(Tune: O sacred head sore wounded.)

1

O Calf so often wounded
Direct your steps to where
His knife is being sharpened
Whose dearest charge you are.
He who devised new crosses
On working men to lay
He'll find a way to butcher
You too some sunny day.

2

In his sight you've found favour
O anxious, panting calf.
It's you above all others
He's claiming for himself.
Just wait in hope, not fretting
Nor try to jump the queue
For now his knife he's whetting
He'll soon be calling you.

3

He has his band of helpers
Of influential men
Who crowd his house and call him
By his familiar name.
These supermen of business
Will take you over, son
They all know all about you
He's praised you to each one.

4

The great industrial captains
Need you for their vast plan.
You have not been forgotten
They want you, little man.
And if, O Calf, you're slaughtered
Then is your glory sure
It shows how well you're thought of
It's what you were made for.

5

So do as you are bidden
And seek no base reward.
More glorious just to whisper
'Lord, I await Thy word.'
He'll bend down to you kindly
And look you in the face

He'll take you round the shambles
And show you your own place.

6
O Calf whom he has chosen
You wandered far and wide
You searched, and failed to find him
And now he's by your side.
After long years he's found you
You've reached your goal at last.
The butcher's arms are round you
He holds you to him fast.

THERE IS NO GREATER CRIME THAN LEAVING

There is no greater crime than leaving.
In friends, what do you count on? Not on what they do.
You never can tell what they will do. Not on what they are.
    That
May change. Only on this: their not leaving.
He who cannot leave cannot stay. He who has a pass
In his pocket – will he stay when the attack begins? Perhaps
He will not stay.
If it goes badly with me, perhaps he will stay. But if it goes
Badly with him, perhaps he will leave.
Fighters are poor people. They cannot leave. When the
    attack
Begins they cannot leave.
He who stays is known. He who left was not known. What left
Is different from what was here.
Before we go into battle I must know: have you a pass
In your coat pocket? Is a plane waiting for you behind the
    battlefield?
How many defeats do you want to survive? Can I send you
    away?
Well, then, let's not go into battle.

WE HAVE MADE A MISTAKE

You are supposed to have said we
Have made a mistake, that's why
You are going to leave us.

You are supposed to have said: if
My eye offends me I
Pluck it out.
By this you were at least suggesting
That you feel linked to us
As a man feels linked
To his eye.

Very good of you, comrade, but
Permit us to point out:
The man in this image, that's us; you
Are only the eye.
And who has ever heard tell of an eye
Simply making off
When the man who owns it makes a mistake?
Where is it going to live?

THE PEASANT'S CONCERN IS WITH HIS FIELD

The peasant's concern is with his field
He looks after his cattle, pays taxes
Produces children, to save on labourers, and
Depends on the price of milk.
The townspeople speak of love for the soil
Of healthy peasant stock and
Call peasants the backbone of the nation.

The townspeople speak of love for the soil
Of healthy peasant stock
And call peasants the backbone of the nation.

The peasant's concern is with his field
He looks after his cattle, pays taxes
Produces children, to save on labourers, and
Depends on the price of milk.

THE FOURTH SONNET

Kindly you had invited him to stay
But had nowhere to entertain your guest.
Before he left he ventured to protest.
In haste he came, in haste he went away.

Did you then have no place for him to be?
The poorest beggar finds his guest some bread.
Here was no need for either house or bed
Only a little shelter by a tree.

Without this he could not feel welcome here.
Coldly received, he thought it best to go.
His presence seemed downright indelicate

And so he lost the courage to be there.
His wishes struck him as unseemly now
And all his haste as inappropriate.

THE SIXTH SONNET

When years ago I tied myself to you
It did not seem the ultimate of bliss.
What you don't want perhaps you never miss
Where lust was slight the grief is trivial too.

Better to feel no grief than too much lust.
And better than to lose, to be resigned.
There's pleasure in not being hurt, men find.
Good if one can; but too bad if one must.

Of course, this is a pretty shabby moral.
He was not rich who never lost a thing.
Nor have I all that much with which to quarrel . . .

I only mean that unattached and free
One may avoid a lot of suffering.
Meanwhile we can't command what is to be.

ON DANTE'S POEMS TO BEATRICE

Even today, above the dusty vault
In which she lies, whom he could never have
Although he dogged her footsteps like a slave
Her name's enough to bring us to a halt.

For he ensured that we should not forget her
Writing such splendid verse to her as made
Us listen to the compliments he paid
Convinced that no one ever put it better.

Dear me, what an abuse he started then
By praising in a manner so arresting
What he had only looked at without testing!

Since he made poems out of glimpses, men
Have seen what looks nice in its street attire
And stays bone-dry, as something to desire.

LONG I HAVE LOOKED FOR THE TRUTH

1

Long I have looked for the truth about the life of people
    together.
That life is crisscrossed, tangled, and difficult to understand.
I have worked hard to understand it and when I had done so
I told the truth as I found it.

2

When I had told the truth that was so difficult to find
It was a common truth, which many told
(And not everyone has such difficulty in finding).

3

Soon after that people arrived in vast masses with pistols
    given to them
And blindly shot around them at all those too poor to wear
    hats
And all those who had told the truth about them and their
    employers
They drove out of the country in the fourteenth year of our
    semi-Republic.

4

From me they took my little house and my car
Which I had earned by hard work.
(I was able to save my furniture.)

5

When I crossed the frontier I thought:
More than my house I need the truth.
But I need my house too. And since then
Truth for me has been like a house and a car.
And they took them.

THE ACTRESS

She being both changeable and constant however
Was not disappointed when she felt different soil beneath her.
If the wind played her enemy and seized her roughly by the
    hair
She just said: that's the hair of many a fellow-creature.

This is Vlassova, the woman you people expelled
Arthur's mother in her red stockings remained crouching.

Even in Oedipus's time she brought him news how few had
    survived
The Widow washed your linen clean in the marshes, to a song.

So I knew everything and in good time made it all plain
And I cried out that you should treat us in this way
And I will show hunger, frost and pain
What they must do to make you go away.

BURIAL OF THE TROUBLE-MAKER IN A ZINC COFFIN

Here in this zinc box
Lies a dead person
Or his legs and his head
Or even less of him
Or nothing, for he was
A trouble-maker.

He was recognised as the root of all evil.
Dig him in. It will be best
If his wife goes alone to the knacker's yard with him
Because anyone else going
Would be a marked man.

What is in that zinc box
Has been egging you on to all sorts of things:
Getting enough to eat
And having somewhere dry to live
And feeding one's children
And insisting on one's exact wages
And solidarity with all
Who are oppressed like yourselves. And
Thinking.

What is in that zinc box said
That another system of production was needed

And that you, the masses of labour in your millions
Must take over.
Until then things won't get better for you.

And because what is in the zinc box said that
It was put into the zinc box and must be dug in
As a trouble-maker who egged you on.
And whoever now talks of getting enough to eat
And whoever of you wants somewhere dry to live
And whoever of you insists on his exact wages
And whoever of you wants to feed his children
And whoever thinks, and proclaims his solidarity
With all who are oppressed –
From now on throughout eternity
He will be put into a zinc box like this one
As a trouble-maker and dug in.

TO THE FIGHTERS IN THE CONCENTRATION CAMPS

You who can hardly be reached
Buried in the concentration camps
Cut off from every human word
Subjected to brutalities
Beaten down but
Not confuted
Vanished but
Not forgotten!

Little as we hear about you, we still hear you are
Incorrigible.
Unteachable, they say, in your commitment to the proletarian
        cause
Unshakably persuaded that there are still in Germany
Two kinds of people, exploiters and exploited
And that the class struggle alone

Can liberate the masses in cities and countryside from their
        misery.
Not by beatings, we hear, nor by hanging can you
Be brought to the point of saying that
Nowadays twice two is five.

So you are
Vanished but
Not forgotten
Beaten down but
Never confuted
Along with all those incorrigibly fighting
Unteachably set on the truth
Now and forever the true
Leaders of Germany.

I NEED NO GRAVESTONE

I need no gravestone, but
If you need one for me
I would like it to bear these words:
He made suggestions. We
Carried them out.
Such an inscription would
Honour us all.

GERMANY

Let others speak of their disgrace.
I am speaking of my own.

O Germany, pale mother
How you sit defiled
Among the peoples!

Among the besmirched
You stand out.

Of your sons the poorest
Lies struck down.
When his hunger was great
Your other sons
Raised their hands against him.
This is now notorious.

With their hands thus raised
Raised against their brother
They stride around insolently before you
And laugh in your face.
This is known.

In your house
Lies are loudly bawled
But truth
Must keep silent.
Is that so?

Why do the oppressors on every side praise you, but
The oppressed indict you?
The exploited
Point their fingers at you, but
The exploiters laud the system
Devised in your house.

And at the same time all see you
Hiding the hem of your skirt, which is bloody
With the blood of your
Best son.

When they hear the speeches issuing from your house, people
        laugh.
But whoever sees you grips his knife
As on seeing a murderess.

O Germany, pale mother
What have your sons done to you
That you sit among the peoples
A mockery or a threat!

WHEN I WAS RICH

For seven weeks of my life I was rich.
With my earnings from a play I bought
A house in a large garden. I had been
Looking over it for more weeks than I lived in it. At different
    times of day
And also of the night, I would walk past to see
How the old trees stood over the lawns in the dawn half-light
Or the pond with its mossy carp on a rainy morning
To see the hedges in the full sun of noon, or
The white rhododendrons in the evening after vespers had
    rung.
Then I and my friends moved in. My car
Was parked under the fir trees. We looked around. There was
    nowhere
You could see all the bounds of the garden from, the slope
    of the lawns
And the clumps of trees prevented the hedges from glimpsing
    one another.
The house too was beautiful. The staircase of noble wood,
    expertly treated
With low risers and wide treads and finely proportioned
    banisters.
The whitewashed rooms had panelled ceilings. Huge iron
    stoves
Elegantly shaped, had scenes chased in the metal: peasants
    at work.
Massive doors led to the cool hall, with its oak tables and
    benches

Their brass handles had been carefully chosen, and the flag-
    stones round the brownish house
Were smooth and worn down under the footsteps
Of earlier inhabitants. What satisfying proportions! Every
    room different
Each better than the last. And how they all changed with the
    time of day!
The changes accompanying the seasons, no doubt exquisite
Were something we did not experience, for
After seven weeks of genuine riches we left the property;
    soon we
Fled over the border.

ON READING 'WHEN I WAS RICH'

The joy of proprietorship was strong in me, and I am glad
To have felt it. To walk through my garden, to have guests
To discuss plans for building, like others of my profession
    before me
This pleased me, I admit it. But now seven weeks seems
    enough.
I left without regret, or with only slight regret. Writing this
I already found it hard to remember. When I ask myself
How many lies I would be ready to tell to keep this property
I know it is not many. Therefore I hope
It was not bad to have this property. It was
Not a small thing, but
There are greater.

v The First Years of Exile
1934–1936

SOLELY BECAUSE OF THE INCREASING DISORDER

Solely because of the increasing disorder
In our cities of class struggle
Some of us have now decided
To speak no more of cities by the sea, snow on roofs, women
The smell of ripe apples in cellars, the senses of the flesh, all
That makes a man round and human
But to speak in future only about the disorder
And so become one-sided, reduced, enmeshed in the business
Of politics and the dry, indecorous vocabulary
Of dialectical economics
So that this awful cramped coexistence
Of snowfalls (they're not merely cold, we know)
Exploitation, the lured flesh, class justice, should not engender
Approval of a world so many-sided; delight in
The contradictions of so bloodstained a life
You understand.

THE SHOPPER

I am an old woman.
When Germany had awoken
Pension rates were cut. My children
Gave me the pennies they could spare. But
I could hardly buy anything now. So at first
I went less often to the shops where I'd gone daily.
But one day I thought it over, and then
Daily once more I went to the baker's, the greengrocer's
As an old customer.
With care I picked my provisions
Took no more than I used to, but no less either
Put rolls beside the loaf and leeks beside the cabbage and only
When they added up the bill did I sigh
With my stiff fingers dug into my little purse
And shaking my head confessed that I didn't have enough

To pay for those few things, and shaking my head I
Left the shop, observed by all the customers.
I said to myself:
If all of us who have nothing
No longer turn up where food is laid out
They may think we don't need anything
But if we come and are unable to buy
They'll know how it is.

THE CHALK CROSS

I am a maidservant. I had an affair
With a man in the SA.
One day before he went off
With a laugh he showed me how they go about
Catching grumblers.
With a stump of chalk from his tunic pocket
He drew a small cross on the palm of his hand.
He told me, with that and in civvies
He'd go to the labour exchanges
Where the unemployed queue up and curse
And would curse with the rest and doing so
As a token of his approval and solidarity
Would pat anyone who cursed on the shoulderblade, where-
        upon the marked man
White cross on his back, would be caught by the SA.
We had a good laugh about that.
I went with him for three months, then I noticed
That he'd taken over my savings book.
He had said he'd keep it for me
Because times were uncertain.
When I challenged him, he swore
That his intentions had been honest. Doing so
He laid his hand on my shoulder to calm me down.
I ran away terrified. At home
I looked at my back in the mirror to see if it didn't bear
A white cross.

THE TOMBSTONE OF THE UNKNOWN
SOLDIER OF THE REVOLUTION

The unknown soldier of the revolution has fallen.
I saw his tombstone in a dream.

It lay in a peat-bog. It consisted of two boulders.
It bore no inscription. But one of the two
Began to speak.

He who lies here, it said, marched
Not to conquer a foreign land, but
His own. Nobody knows
What his name is. But the history books
Give the names of those who vanquished him.

Because he wanted to live like a human being
He was slaughtered like a savage beast.

His last words were a whisper
For they came from a strangled throat, but
The cold wind carried them everywhere
To many freezing people.

THE DYING POET'S ADDRESS TO
YOUNG PEOPLE

You young people of times to come
And of new dawns over cities which
Have yet to be built, also you
Who are still unborn, listen
To my voice, the voice of a man who died
And not gloriously.

But
Like a farmer who has not tended his land

And like a lazy carpenter who ran away
Leaving the rafters uncovered.

Thus did I
Waste my time, squander my days and now
I must ask you
To say everything that was not said
To do everything that was not done, and quickly
To forget me, please, so that
My bad example does not lead you astray.

Ah why did I
Sit down at table with those who produced nothing
And share the meal which they had not prepared?

Ah why did I mix
My best sayings with their
Idle chatter? While outside
Unschooled people were walking around
Thirsty for instruction.

Ah why
Do my songs not rise from the places where
The cities are nourished, where they build ships, why
Do they not rise from the fast moving
Locomotives like smoke which
Stays behind in the sky?

Because for people who create and are useful
My talk
Is like ashes in the mouth and a drunken mumbling.

Not a single word
Can I offer you, you generations of times to come
Not one indication could I give, pointing
With my uncertain finger, for how could anyone
Show the way who has not
Travelled it himself?

So all I can do, who have thus
Wasted my life, is tell you
To obey not a single command that comes
From our rotten mouths and to take
No advice from those
Who have failed so badly, but
To decide for yourselves what is good for you
And what will help you
To cultivate the land which we let go to ruin, and
To make the cities
Which we poisoned
Places for people to live in.

UNITED FRONT SONG

1

And because a man is human
He'll want to eat, and thanks a lot
But talk can't take the place of meat
Or fill an empty pot.
 So left, two, three!
 So left, two, three!
 Comrade, there's a place for you.
 Take your stand in the workers' united front
 For you are a worker too.

2

And because a man is human
He won't care for a kick in the face.
He doesn't want slaves under him
Or above him a ruling class.
 So left, two, three!
 So left, two, three!
 Comrade, there's a place for you.
 Take your stand in the workers' united front
 For you are a worker too.

3

And because a worker's a worker
No one else will bring him liberty.
It's nobody's work but the workers' own
To set the worker free.
  So left, two, three!
  So left, two, three!
  Comrade, there's a place for you.
  Take your stand in the workers' united front
  For you are a worker too.

THE HELL OF THE DISENCHANTERS

Leaving behind the hell of the disenchanted
We came to the hell of the disenchanters.
In a grey city, filled with market cries
We met those who had no faces left.

Whoever we met looked away.
Whoever we followed put on speed. We however saw
Them dressed in cheap and dear clothing, old
And young persons, of both sexes.

Still to be seen was many a
Trace of former beauty, capable no doubt of seduction –
Clever foreheads and – most shattering of all – relics of
An honest smile.

Those who had crumbled under threats
Still had much the same way of holding their heads
As those who are not to be cowed.
Those who once had said: 'If I say I'm coming I'll come' –
Of course nobody expects them any longer, but
They still thread their way quickly through the mob.

They are now entirely on their own, yet still involved
In hazardous enterprises. Peering into offices from the outside

We watched them show one another their letters of credit
And point at the many stamps and signatures
Using their thumb to cover the places
Where the year had been scratched out.

BUYING ORANGES

In yellow fog along Southampton Street
Suddenly a fruit barrow, and an old hag
Beneath a lamp, fingering a paper bag.
I stood surprised and dumb like one who sees
What he's been after, right before his eyes.

Oranges! Always oranges as of old!
I blew into my hands against the cold
And searched my pockets for a coin to buy.

But while I clutched the pennies in my hand
Looked at the price and saw it written down
With grubby crayon on some newspaper
I saw that I was softly whistling, and
At once the bitter truth was all too clear:
That you are not here with me in this town.

QUESTIONS

Write me what you're wearing. Are you warm?
Write me how you sleep. Is your bed soft?
Write me how you look. Are you the same?
Write me what you miss. Is it my arm?

Tell me: are they letting you alone?
Can you hold out? What will their next move be?
What are you doing? Is it what should be done?
What are you thinking of? Is it of me?

Questions are all that I can give you, and
I take what answers come, because I must.
If you are tired, I can't give you a hand;
Or, hungry, feed you. Thus, it is as though
I were not in the world, did not exist.
It is as though I had forgotten you.

THE CALEDONIAN MARKET

I
Under Troy lie seven cities.
Someone dug the whole lot up again.
Are seven cities buried under London?
Is this where they sell off the bottommost remains?

By the stall with the phosphorescent fish
Underneath old socks you see a hat.
Yer won't get a new one under seven bob, tosh
And this one's just a florin and not too bad at that.

II
The frightful god sat eternally, the soles of his feet pointing
    outwards
Then one day his nose broke, a toe came off, and his menacing
    arm
But the bronze body was too heavy, just the hand went travel-
    ling downwards
From the thief's to the Caledonian Market, through many
    living hands.

III

'Oh, East is East and West is West!'
Their hireling minstrel cried.
But I observed with interest
Bridges across that great divide
And huge guns trundling East I've seen
And cheerful troops keeping them clean.
Meanwhile, from East to West, back rolled
Tea soaked in blood, war wounded, gold.

And the Widow at Windsor, all dressed in black
Grins, takes the money, stuffs it in her pocket
And gives the wounded a pat on the back
And sends them down to the Caledonian Market.
Their walk may have lost its spring, but they try
To hobble around the stalls and buy
A second-hand wooden leg instead
To match their equally wooden head.

SPEECH TO DANISH WORKING-CLASS ACTORS ON THE ART OF OBSERVATION

Hither you have come to appear on the stage, but first
You must tell us: what is the point?
You have come to show yourselves before the public
And what you can do, in short to be put on view
As something worth seeing . . .
And the public, you hope
Will give you applause as you sweep them away
From their narrow world into your broad one, allowing them
        to enjoy
Vertigo on the summit ridge, the passions at their
Fullest strength. And now you are asked: what is the point?

For down here, on the lower benches
Your spectators have started disputing: obstinately

Some of them insist you should
On no account show yourselves only but
The world. What's the good, they say
Of our once again being enabled to see how this man
Can be sad, or this woman heartless, or what sort of
Wicked monarch that man at the back can portray? What is
     the point
Of this continual presentation of the postures and grimaces
Of a handful of people relentlessly gripped by Fate?

All you put before us is victims, acting yourselves
Like helpless victims of inner impulses and outside powers.
They receive their pleasures like dogs, tossed to them by
     unseen
Hands like unexpected crusts, and just as
Unexpected the nooses drop around their necks, the cares
     which
Fall from above. But we, the spectators
On the lower benches, sit with glassy eyes and goggle
Fixed in your grip, at your grimaces and convulsions
Sensing at second hand the proffered pleasure and
Uncontrollable care.

No, we cry from the lower benches in our discontent
Enough! That will not do. Have you really
Not yet heard it is now common knowledge
That this net was knotted and cast by men?
Today everywhere, from the hundred-storeyed cities
Over the seas, cross-ploughed by teeming liners
To the loneliest villages, the word has spread
That mankind's fate is man alone. Therefore
We now ask you, the actors
Of our time – a time of overthrow and of boundless mastery
Of all nature, even men's own – at last
To change yourselves and show us mankind's world
As it really is: made by men and open to alteration.

That, roughly, is what comes from the benches. Of course
    not all
Their occupants agree. With drooping shoulders
The majority sit hunched, their foreheads furrowed like
Stony ground that has been repeatedly ploughed-up to no
    purpose. Exhausted
By the unceasing struggles of their daily life they await with
    greed
Just what repels the others. A little massage
For their flaccid spirits. A little tautening
Of slackened nerves. Cheap adventures, a sense of magic
    hands
Bearing them off from a world they cannot master
And have had to give up. So which of your spectators
Should you follow, actors? I would suggest
The discontented.

But how to get this going? How
To portray men's living together like this so
That it becomes possible to understand and master it? How
To show not only oneself, and others not only
As they conduct themselves once
The net has caught them? How
Now to show the knotting and casting of fate's net?
And that it has been knotted and cast by men? The first thing
You have to learn is the *art of observation*.

You, actor
Must master the art of observation
Before all other arts.

For what matters is not how you look but
What you have seen and can show us. What's worth knowing
Is what you know.
People will observe you to see
How well you have observed.

The man who only observes himself however never gains
Knowledge of men. He is too anxious
To hide himself from himself. And nobody is
Cleverer than he himself is.

So your schooling must begin among
Living people. Let your first school
Be your place of work, your dwelling, your part of the town.
Be the street, the underground, the shops. You should
    observe
All the people there, strangers as if they were acquaintances,
    but
Acquaintances as if they were strangers to you.

There stands the man who is paying his taxes; he is not like
Every man who pays taxes, even though
Everyone pays them with reluctance. Indeed
When engaged on this business he is not always like himself.
And the man who collects those taxes:
Is he really quite different from the man who pays them?
He not only pays taxes himself but has other points
In common with the man he is pestering. And that woman
    there
Didn't always speak so harshly, nor is that other woman
Charming to one and all. And the assertive guest –
Is he merely assertive, is he not also full of fear?
Then that dispirited woman who has no shoes for her child –
Were not empires won just with the shreds of her spirit?
Look, she is pregnant once more. And have you seen a sick
Man's expression when he learns that he will never get well?
But that he would be well if he didn't
Have to work? Look at him now, spending
The remains of his time leafing through the book that tells
How one might make an inhabitable planet of the world.
Nor should you forget the pictures on screen and newspaper
    page.
See how they walk and speak, those rulers

Who hold the threads of your fate in their white and brutal
      hands.
You should inspect such people exactly. And now
Imagine all that is going on around you, all those struggles
Picturing them just like historical incidents
For this is how you should go on to portray them on the
      stage:
The fight for a job, sweet and bitter conversations
Between the man and his woman, arguments about books
Resignation and revolt, attempt and failure
All these you will go on to portray as historical incidents.
(Even what is happening here, at this moment, with us, is
      something you
Can regard as a picture in this way: how the refugee
Playwright instructs you in the
Art of observation.)

In order to observe
One must learn how to compare. In order to compare
One must have observed. By means of observation
Knowledge is generated; on the other hand knowledge is
      needed
For observation. And
He observes badly who does not know
How to use what he has observed. The fruitgrower
Inspects the appletree with a keener eye than does the walker
But no one can see man exactly unless he knows it is
Man who is the fate of man.

The art of observation
Applied to man is but a branch of the
Art of dealing with men. Your task, actors, is to be
Explorers and teachers of the art of dealing with people.
Knowing their nature and demonstrating it you teach them
To deal with themselves. You teach them the great art
Of living together.

Yes, I hear you say, but how are we
Downtrodden and harassed, exploited and dependent
Kept in ignorance, living insecurely
To adopt that splendid attitude of explorers and pioneers
Who reconnoitre a strange country with a view to exploiting
          it and
Subjecting it to themselves? After all we were never more than
The object of dealings by others more fortunate. How
Are we, never more than the
Trees that bore the fruit, suddenly to become the gardeners?
          Just that
Seems to me the art you must learn, who are actors
And workers at the same time.

Nothing can be impossible
To learn if it is of use. No one develops his observation better
Than you do in your daily jobs. Recognising the foreman's
Weaknesses and abilities, exactly weighing
Your colleagues' habits and modes of thought
Is useful to you. How is
Your class struggle to be waged without
Knowledge of men? I see you
All the best among you, greedily snatching at awareness
The knowledge which sharpens observation and leads in turn to
New knowledge. And already
Many of you are studying the laws of men's life together,
          already
Your class is determined to master its problems and thereby
The problems of
All mankind. And that is where you
The workers' actors, as you learn and teach
Can play your part creatively in all the struggles
Of men of your time, thereby
Helping, with the seriousness of study and the cheerfulness
          of knowledge
To turn the struggle into common experience and
Justice into a passion.

Five Children's Songs

Adolf Hitler's facial hair
Is a curious affair.
It's what I'd call uncouth:
So small a toothbrush for so big a mouth.

Balthasar made saucepan lids
He had 27 kids
They put the lids on sale
And lived on an unprincely scale.

Christine's apron, if you please
Finished high above her knees
Back to front, as if it were
One of those collars sailors wear.

Doctors of Philosophy
Have problems now in Germany.
Where moon and stars have left the sky
A candle's all they can read by.

Events cast shadows long before.
One such event would be a war.
But how are shadows to be seen
When total darkness fills the screen?

Ford he made a motor car.
Its raucous noise can sometimes jar.
The hood can sometimes come apart
And it doesn't always start.

Gratitude's a useful term:
Give thanks for what by rights you earn.

The upper class use it a lot
Their servants somehow not.

Hindenburg was incompetent
And so he lost his war.
The Germans said: make him President
That's what he's fittest for.

India's a land of wonders
Which England freely plunders.
Those born in India
Can assume they'll be skinned there.

Kittens are often done away with
Before they're old enough to play with.
They're put in a bucket
And then they kick it.

Luise cries so frequently
The gardener dug her a pond for free
To catch her tears. Soon it was brimming
With, in the middle, a frog swimming.

Marie stood upon a mound
Feeling frightened of a hound.
The hound felt frightened of Marie
Because she screamed so frighteningly.

Nosy Gladys
Found a radish
In her aunt's pianoforte.
She kept it. Naughty!

Overhead, in Heaven
Observe God being driven
By a horse with a whip.
The horse cries: gee up!

Presents
Are something no one resents
At Christmas, e.g., Easter, one's birthday . . . But who gets
  one
At Whitsun?

Quanglewangles in the night
Are not a nice sight.
Those who spot them
Shouldn't swat them.

Rich man and his poorer brother
Stood and looked at one another
Till the poor one softly swore:
You'd not be rich if I weren't poor.

Steff sits in the bog so long
Because he takes a book along.
If the book is thick
He'll be out some time next week.

Tom has a wooden hat.
He's very proud of that.
He put a pastryboard on the piano top
And sawed it up.

Uncle's watch is a good make
So please don't throw it in the lake
Because it cannot swim
And tells the time to him.

Violets should be arranged
In vases, and their water changed.
Suppose the cow gets there first
It will eat them up and burst.

Whales tell one another
When bitter their cup:

If you ain't no blubber
You won't get cut up.

Xantippe said to Socrates:
You're drunk, just look at you.
He said: one must doubt what one sees
Nothing is wholly true.
He ranks as a philosopher
She as the classic shrew.

Ypres on the Flanders plain
1917
A lot of those who'd seen
That city never saw again.

Zebras climbing up a ladder
The first of them looks fatter
The second not so fat.
The ladder falls down flat.

THE CHILD WHO DIDN'T WANT TO WASH

Once there was a child
That didn't want to wash.
They washed it and, behold
It rubbed its face in ash.

The Kaiser came to call
Up seven flights of stairs.
Mother looked for a towel
To wipe its face and hair.

The towel had been mislaid.
The whole visit was wrecked.
The Kaiser went away.
What could the child expect?

THE PLUM TREE

The plum tree in the yard's so small
It's hardly like a tree at all.
Yet there it is, railed round
To keep it safe and sound.

The poor thing can't grow any more
Though if it could it would for sure.
There's nothing to be done
It gets too little sun.

The plum tree never bears a plum
So it's not easy to believe.
It is a plum tree all the same
One tells it by the leaf.

THE TAILOR OF ULM
(*Ulm 1592*)

Bishop, I can fly
Said the tailor to the bishop.
Just watch me try!
And with a couple of things
That looked like wings
To the big, big roof of the church he climbed.

The bishop walked by.
It's nothing but a lie
A man is not a bird
No man will ever fly
Said the bishop of the tailor.

The tailor has passed away
Said the people to the bishop
A farcical affair.

Broken-winged he crashed
And now lies smashed
On the hard, hard city square.

Let the church bells ring
It was nothing but a lie
A man is not a bird
No man will ever fly
Said the bishop to the people.

THE ROBBER AND HIS SERVANT

Two robbers were plundering the province of Hesse
Many a peasant's neck they broke
One was as thin as a hungry wolf
And the other as fat as the pope.

But what made their bodies so different?
It's because they were servant and master.
The master swigged the cream off the milk, so then
The servant got his milk already sour.

The peasants caught the robbers
And when they hung by *one* rope
One hung there as thin as a hungry wolf
And one as fat as the pope.

The peasants stood there crossing themselves
And staring at the two
They saw that the fat man was a robber
But why was the thin man one too?

WHEN THE MIGHTY BANDITS
CAME

When the mighty bandits came
I opened the doorway wide
And I heard them call my name
And I stepped outside.

No demand had yet been stated
When I fetched the keys
So no crimes were perpetrated
Just discoveries.

REPORT FROM GERMANY

We learn that in Germany
In the days of the brown plague
On the roof of an engineering works suddenly
A red flag fluttered in the November wind
The outlawed flag of freedom!
In the grey mid-November from the sky
Fell rain mixed with snow
It was the 7th, though: day of the Revolution!

And look! the red flag!

The workers stand in the yards
Shield their eyes with their hands and stare
At the roof through the flurries of icy rain.

Then lorries roll up filled with stormtroopers
And they drive to the wall any who wear work clothes
And with cords bind any fists that are calloused
And from the sheds after their interrogation
Stumble the beaten and bloody
Not one of whom has named the man
Who was on the roof.

So they drive away those who kept silent
And the rest have had enough.
But next day there waves again
The red flag of the proletariat
On the engineering works roof. Again
Thuds through the dead-still town
The stormtroopers' tread. In the yards
There are no men to be seen now. Only women
Stand with stony faces; hands shielding their eyes, they gaze
At the roof through the flurries of icy rain.

And the beatings begin once more. Under interrogation
The women testify: that flag
Is a bedsheet in which
We bore away one who died yesterday.
You can't blame us for the colour it is.
It is red with the murdered man's blood, you should know.

THE LAST WISH

In Altona, when they raided the working-class districts
They caught four of our people. For their execution
Seventy-five were dragged along to watch.
This is what they saw: the youngest, a big chap, when asked
His last wish (in line with standard procedure)
Drily said he wanted once more to stretch his limbs.
Freed from his bonds, he stretched and with both fists
Hit the Nazi commander on the chin
With all his strength. After which they strapped him
To the narrow board, face upwards, and cut
His head off.

WHEN EVIL-DOING COMES LIKE FALLING RAIN

Like one who brings an important letter to the counter after
     office hours: the counter is already closed.
Like one who seeks to warn the city of an impending flood,
     but speaks another language. They do not understand
     him.
Like a beggar who knocks for the fifth time at a door where
     he has four times been given something: the fifth
     time he is hungry.
Like one whose blood flows from a wound and who awaits
     the doctor: his blood goes on flowing.

So do we come forward and report that evil has been done us.

The first time it was reported that our friends were being
     butchered there was a cry of horror. Then a hundred
     were butchered. But when a thousand were butchered
     and there was no end to the butchery, a blanket of
     silence spread.

When evil-doing comes like falling rain, nobody calls out
     'stop!'

When crimes begin to pile up they become invisible. When
     sufferings become unendurable the cries are no longer
     heard. The cries, too, fall like rain in summer.

TO A WAVERER

You tell us
It looks bad for our cause.
The darkness gets deeper. The powers get less.
Now, after we worked for so many years
We are in a more difficult position than at the start.

But the enemy stands there, stronger than ever before.
His powers appear to have grown. He has taken on an aspect
        of invincibility.
We however have made mistakes; there is no denying it.
Our numbers are dwindling.
Our slogans are in disarray. The enemy has twisted
Part of our words beyond recognition.

What is now false of what we said:
Some or all?
Whom do we still count on? Are we just left over, thrown out
Of the living stream? Shall we remain behind
Understanding no one and understood by none?

Have we got to be lucky?

This you ask. Expect
No other answer than your own.

THE MOSCOW WORKERS TAKE POSSESSION OF THE GREAT METRO ON APRIL 27, 1935

We were told: 80,000 workers
Built the Metro, many after a day's work elsewhere
Sometimes all through the night. This past year
Young men and girls were always seen
Laughing as they climbed out of the tunnels, proudly flaunting
Their work clothes, mud-caked and drenched with sweat.
All obstacles –
Underground streams, pressure from multi-storey buildings
Massive cave-ins – were overcome. For the ornamentation
No pains were spared. The best marble
Was transported from afar, the finest woods
Worked with scrupulous care. The splendid trains
Ran almost soundlessly at last
Through tunnels light as day: for exacting clients
The best of everything.

Now that the railway was built in accordance with the most
      perfect plans
And the owners came to view it and
To ride on it, they were the selfsame people
Who had built it.
Thousands of them were there, walking about
Examining the giant halls, while in the trains
Great multitudes went riding past, their faces –
Men, women and children, greybeards as well –
Turned to the stations, beaming as if at the theatre, for the
      stations
Were all built differently, of different stone
In different styles; the light also
Came each time from a different source. Anyone getting
      aboard
Was shoved to the back in the cheerful crush
Since the seats up front were
Best for viewing the stations. At every station
The children were lifted up. As often as possible
The travellers rushed out and inspected
With eager, exacting eyes the finished job. They felt the pillars
And appraised their gloss. They scraped the soles of their
      shoes
Over the stone floors, to see if the slabs
Were smoothly fitted. Crowding back into the cars
They tested the wall surfaces and fingered
The glass. Men and women were continually
Pointing out – uncertain if they were the right ones –
Places where they had worked: the stone
Bore the imprint of their hands. Each face
Was distinctly visible, for there was much light
Many bulbs, more than in any railway I have seen.
The tunnels also were lighted, not one metre of labour
Went unlit. And all this
Had been built in a single year and by so many workmen
Unique among the railways of the world. And no
Other railway in the world had ever had so many owners.

For this wonder of construction was witnessing
What none of its predecessors in the cities of many centuries
Had witnessed: *the builders in the role of proprietors.*
Where would it ever have happened that the fruits of labour
Fell to those who had laboured? Where in all time
Were the people who had put up a building
Not always turned out of it?
When we saw them riding in their trains
The work of their own hands, we knew:
This is the grand picture that once upon a time
Rocked the classic writers who foresaw it.

RECOMMENDATION TO TRETIAKOFF
TO GET WELL

A sick man's argument
Is a thing to be laughed about.

Eat an extra meal and eat it slowly
Thinking of your enemies
Sleep till late in the day
And they shall lose their sleep.

In the interest of the Soviets
Drink a glass of milk mornings
So that your advice to us shall not be
The advice of a sick man.

Swim in the lake, for pleasure. The water
Which could drown you
Buoys you up.
Swimming you cleave it, behind you
It comes together again.

IN THE SECOND YEAR OF MY FLIGHT

In the second year of my flight
I read in a paper, in a foreign language
That I had lost my citizenship.
I was not sad and not pleased
When I read my name among many others
Both good and bad.
The plight of those who had fled seemed no worse to me than
The plight of those who stayed.

BALLAD OF MARIE SANDERS, THE JEW'S WHORE

1

In Nuremberg they made a law
At which many a woman wept who'd
Lain in bed with the wrong man.
  'The price is rising for butcher's meat.
  The drumming's now at its height.
  God alive, if they are coming down our street
  It'll be tonight.'

2

Marie Sanders, your lover's
Hair is too black.
Take our advice, and don't you be to him
What you were yesterday.
  'The price is rising for butcher's meat.
  The drumming's now at its height.
  God alive, if they are coming down our street
  It'll be tonight.'

3

Mother, give me the latchkey
It can't be so bad
The moon's the same as ever.

'The price is rising for butcher's meat.
The drumming's now at its height.
God alive, if they are coming down our street
It'll be tonight.'

4

One morning, close on nine
She was driven through the town
In her slip, round her neck a sign, her hair all shaven.
The street was yelling. She
Coldly stared.
　'The price is rising for butcher's meat.
　And Streicher's speaking tonight.
　God alive, if we'd an ear to hear his speech
　We would start to make sense of our plight.'

QUESTIONS FROM A WORKER WHO READS

Who built Thebes of the seven gates?
In the books you will find the names of kings.
Did the kings haul up the lumps of rock?
And Babylon, many times demolished
Who raised it up so many times? In what houses
Of gold-glittering Lima did the builders live?
Where, the evening that the Wall of China was finished
Did the masons go? Great Rome
Is full of triumphal arches. Who erected them? Over whom
Did the Caesars triumph? Had Byzantium, much praised in song
Only palaces for its inhabitants? Even in fabled Atlantis
The night the ocean engulfed it
The drowning still bawled for their slaves.

The young Alexander conquered India.
Was he alone?
Caesar beat the Gauls.
Did he not have even a cook with him?

Philip of Spain wept when his armada
Went down. Was he the only one to weep?
Frederick the Second won the Seven Years' War. Who
Else won it?

Every page a victory.
Who cooked the feast for the victors?
Every ten years a great man.
Who paid the bill?

So many reports.
So many questions.

THE SHOE OF EMPEDOCLES

1
When Empedocles of Agrigentum
Had gained the admiration of his fellow citizens along with
The infirmities of age
He decided to die. But since he loved
A certain few by whom he, in turn, was loved
He did not wish to perish in front of them, but
Rather to disappear.
He invited them to go on an excursion, not all of them
One or another he omitted so that in the choice
And in the collective undertaking
Chance played a part.
They climbed Aetna.
The difficulty of the climb
Exacted silence. No one missed
Wise words. At the top
They stretched out to get their breath
Busy with the view, glad to have reached their goal.
Unnoticed the teacher left them.
As they began to speak again, at first they noticed
Nothing, only later

Here and there a word was missing and they looked around
  for him.
But long before he had already gone to the crater
Not hurrying very fast. Once he stood still and he heard
How far off behind the crater
The talk arose again. Individual words
Could no longer be made out: dying had begun.
As he stood at the crater
His face turned away, wishing to know no more of what
No longer concerned him in the distance, the old man bent
  slowly
Carefully slipped a shoe from one foot and, smiling
Tossed it a few paces to one side, so that it would not
Be found too quickly but yet at the right time, that is
Before it had rotted. Only then
Did he go to the crater. When his friends
Returned without him, having looked for him
Gradually through the next weeks and months
His death began, as he had wished it. There were some
Who still waited for him, while others
Gave him up for dead. Some of them held
Their questions back, awaiting his return, while others
Sought the solution themselves. Slowly as the clouds
Withdraw into the sky, unchanged, only growing smaller
And more delicate while you do not look back, more distant
When you seek them again, perhaps already mixed with others
Thus he withdrew from their ordinary affairs in the ordinary
  way.
Then a rumour arose.
He could not be dead, for he had been immortal, so it went.
Mystery surrounded him. It was considered possible
That there was something beyond the earthly which modified
The course of human events for the individual, this kind of
  babble arose.
But at this time his shoe was found, the leather shoe
Tangible, worn, earthly! Left behind for those who
When they no longer see, immediately begin to believe.

His last days
Became real once more. He had died like anyone else.

2
Others might have described the foregoing
Differently: this Empedocles
Had really sought to insure himself worship as a god
And by a secret disappearance, a sly
Leap into Aetna without witnesses, to found a legend
That he was not of human stuff, not subject to the laws
Of dissolution. And in this
His shoe played a trick on him by falling into men's hands.
(Consequently some say the crater itself, angered
By such an affair, had simply spewed up the shoes
Of the corrupt one.) But we would rather believe:
If he did not really remove his shoe, he had merely
Forgotten our stupidity and not thought how we hasten
To make obscurity more obscure and prefer to believe
The absurd rather than to seek for a sufficient cause. And
        anyway the mountain
Certainly did not get angry over such carelessness or because
It believed the man wished to delude us into paying him
        divine honours
(For the mountain believes nothing and is not concerned with
        us)
But merely spewing fire as it always did it threw up the shoe
For us and so, when the scholars were busy scenting a mystery
Developing profound metaphysics, in fact all too busy
Suddenly they were confounded by holding the shoe of the
        teacher in their hands, the tangible shoe
Worn, made of leather, earthly.

ON TEACHING WITHOUT PUPILS

Teaching without pupils
Writing without fame
Are difficult.

It is good to go out in the morning
With your newly written pages
To the waiting printer, across the buzzing market
Where they sell meat and workmen's tools:
You sell sentences.

The driver has driven fast
He has not breakfasted
Every bend was a risk
In haste he steps through the doorway:
The man he came to fetch
Has already gone.

There speaks the man to whom no one is listening:
He speaks too loud
He repeats himself
He says things that are wrong:
He goes uncorrected.

THE LEARNER

First I built on sand, then I built on rock.
When the rock caved in
I no longer built on anything.
Then I often built again
On sand and rock, as it came, but
I had learned.

Those to whom I had entrusted the letter
Threw it away. But those I paid no attention to
Brought it back to me.
Thereby I learned.

What I ordered was not carried out.
When I arrived I saw
It was wrong. The right thing

Had been done.
From that I learned.

The scars are painful
Now it is cold.
But I often said: only the grave
Will have nothing more to teach me.

THE PASSENGER

When, years ago, I learned
To steer a car, my teacher made me
Smoke a cigar, and if it went out
In heavy traffic or on sharp corners
He relieved me of the wheel. Also
He told jokes as I drove, and if
Too occupied with steering, I did not laugh, he took
The wheel from me. I feel unsafe, he said.
I, the passenger, am frightened when I see
The driver of the car too preoccupied
With driving.

Since then, when working
I take care not to get too absorbed in the work.
I pay attention to all sorts of things around me
Often I interrupt my work to talk to someone.
Driving too fast to be able to smoke
Is a habit I've got out of. I think of
The passenger.

THE PLAYWRIGHT'S SONG

I am a playwright. I show
What I have seen. In the man markets
I have seen how men are traded. That
I show, I, the playwright.

How they step into each other's rooms with schemes
Or rubber truncheons, or with cash
How they stand in the streets and wait
How they lay traps for one another
Full of hope
How they make appointments
How they hang each other
How they make love
How they defend their loot
How they eat
I show all that.

The words which they call out to each other I report.
What the mother says to her son
What the employer tells the employee
What the wife replies to her husband
All the begging words, all the commanding
The grovelling, the misleading
The lying, the unknowing
The winning, the wounding . . .
I report them all.

I see snowstorms making their entrances
I see earthquakes coming forward
I see mountains blocking the road
And rivers I see breaking their banks.
But the snowstorms have hats on
The earthquakes have money in their wallet
The mountains came in a conveyance
And the headlong rivers control the police.
That I reveal.

To learn how to show what I see
I read up the representations of other peoples and other
        periods.
One or two plays I have adapted, precisely
Checking the technique of those times and absorbing

Whatever is of use to me.
I studied the portrayal of the great feudal figures
By the English, of rich individuals
To whom the world existed for their fuller development.
I studied the moralising Spaniards
The Indians, masters of beautiful sensations
And the Chinese, who portray the family
And the many-coloured destinies found in cities.

And so swiftly did the appearance of cities and houses
Change in my time that to go away for two years
And come back was like a trip to another city
And people in vast numbers changed their appearance
Within a few years. I saw
Workers enter the factory gates, and the gateway was tall
But when they came out they had to bend.
Then I told myself:
Everything alters and is for its own time only.

And so I gave each setting its recognition mark
And branded the figures of the year on each factory yard and
        each room
Like drovers who brand figures on their cattle to identify
        them.
And the sentences too that were spoken there
I gave recognition marks to, so that they became like the
        sayings
Of impermanent men which are set down
So that they may not be forgotten.

What the woman in overalls said during those years
Bent over her leaflets
And the way the brokers used yesterday to speak to their
        clerks
Hats on the backs of their heads
I marked with the impermanence of
Their year of origin.

But all this I yielded up to astonishment
Even the most familiar part of it.
That a mother gave her child the breast
I reported like something no one would believe.
That a porter slammed the door in a freezing man's face
Like somebody nobody had ever seen.

LETTER TO THE PLAYWRIGHT ODETS

Comrade, in your play Paradise Lost you show
That the families of the exploiters
Are destroyed in the end.
What do you mean by that?

It could be that the families of the exploiters
Are destroyed. But what if they're not?
Do they cease to exploit when they go to pieces or
Is it easier for us to be exploited so long
As they've not gone to pieces? Should the hungry man
Continue to be hungry, so long as he who refuses him bread
Is a healthy man?

Or do you mean to tell us that our exploiters
Have already been weakened? Should we
Just sit there, waiting? Such pictures
Our house painter painted, comrade, and overnight
We felt the strength of our exploiters who'd gone to pieces.

Or should you feel sorry for them? Should we
Burst into tears when we see the bedbugs move out?
You, comrade, who showed compassion towards the man
Who has nothing to eat, do you now feel compassion
For the man who has stuffed himself sick?

HOW THE SHIP 'OSKAWA' WAS BROKEN UP BY
HER OWN CREW

'Early in 1922
I signed on the 6000 ton freighter *Oskawa*
Built four years earlier for two million dollars
By the United States Shipping Board. In Hamburg
We picked up cargo, champagne and liqueurs for Rio.
As the pay was bad
We felt a need to drown our sorrows
In alcohol. So
A case or two of champagne found its way into
The crew's quarters. But from the officers' room too
Even on the bridge and in the chart-room
Only four days after leaving Hamburg, were heard
The clinking of glasses and the songs
Of carefree folk. Several times
The ship was thrown off her course. However
Owing to sundry favourable circumstances
We reached Rio de Janeiro. Our skipper
Missed a hundred cases of champagne
When we unloaded. But as he could not pick up any better
Crew in Brazil he had to
Make do with us. We loaded
Over a thousand tons of frozen meat for Hamburg.
A day or so out, our sorrows overcame us again –
The bad pay, our insecure old age – and
One of us in his despair fed
Far too much oil into the furnace, and fire
Shot from the funnel all over the upper structure so
That lifeboats, bridge and chart-room were burned away.
        To prevent our sinking
We helped put it out, but
Meditating on the bad pay (uncertain prospects) didn't
Exert ourselves very hard to save much from the deck. It
Could easily be repaired at some cost; after all, they had
Saved enough on our pay.

Undue exertion in middle life
Ages men fast, unfits them for life's struggle.
So, as we had to be sparing of our strength
The dynamos burned out one fine day, since they needed
      the sort of care
Not given by those with no heart in the job. Now
We had no light. At first we used oil lamps
To avoid collision with other ships, but
A tired mate, dejected by thoughts
Of his joyless old age, threw the lamps overboard
To save work. About then, just off Madeira
The meat began to stink in the cold storage chamber
Due to the failure of the dynamos. Unfortunately
A preoccupied sailor, instead of the bilges
Pumped out nearly all the fresh water. There was enough
      left for drinking
But none for the boilers. So we had to
Use salt water for steam, with the result that
The pipes were choked with salt. Cleaning them out
Took quite a while. It had to be done seven times.
Then there was a breakdown in the engine room. Grinning
We patched it up again. The *Oskawa*
Limped slowly into Madeira. No facilities there
For the extensive repairs that were now needed. We procured
Only water and a few more lamps and some oil for the
      running-lights. The dynamos
It appeared, were totally ruined, consequently
The refrigeration system didn't work, and the stench of
The frozen meat rotting became intolerable to
Our shattered nerves. The skipper
Never stirred without his revolver – a sign of
Insulting mistrust. One of us, outraged
By such demeaning treatment
Finally shot steam into the refrigerator pipes, so that the
      damn meat
Should at least be cooked. That afternoon
The whole crew sat down and diligently figured

How much the United States Government would have to
      pay for the cargo. Before the voyage ended
We actually managed to beat our own record: off the coast of
      Holland
The fuel-oil supply suddenly gave out, and we had to be
Towed into Hamburg at enormous expense.
The stinking meat caused our skipper much further trouble.
      The ship went
To the boneyard. Any child, we considered
Could see from this that our pay
Really was too low.'

YEARS AGO WHEN I

Years ago when I was studying the ways of the Chicago
      Wheat Exchange
I suddenly grasped how they managed the whole world's
      wheat there
And yet I did not grasp it either and lowered the book
I knew at once: you've run
Into bad trouble.

There was no feeling of enmity in me and it was not the
      injustice
Frightened me, only the thought that
Their way of going about it won't do
Filled me completely.

These people, I saw, lived by the harm
Which they did, not by the good.
This was a situation, I saw, that could only be maintained
By crime because too bad for most people.
In this way every
Achievement of reason, invention or discovery
Must lead only to still greater wretchedness.

Such and suchlike I thought at that moment
Far from anger or lamenting, as I lowered the book
With its description of the Chicago wheat market and
    exchange.

Much trouble and tribulation
Awaited me.

WHY SHOULD MY NAME BE MENTIONED?

1

Once I thought: in distant times
When the buildings have collapsed in which I live
And the ships have rotted in which I travelled
My name will still be mentioned
With others.

2

Because I praised the useful, which
In my day was considered base
Because I battled against all religions
Because I fought oppression or
For another reason.

3

Because I was for people and
Entrusted everything to them, thereby honouring them
Because I wrote verses and enriched the language
Because I taught practical behaviour or
For some other reason.

4

Therefore I thought my name would still be
Mentioned; on a stone
My name would stand; from books
It would get printed into the new books.

5
But today
I accept that it will be forgotten.
Why
Should the baker be asked for if there is enough bread?
Why
Should the snow be praised that has melted
If new snowfalls are impending?
Why
Should there be a past if
There is a future?

6
Why
Should my name be mentioned?

VI Later Svendborg Poems and Satires
1936–1938

GERMAN SONG

Once more they're saying a great age will dawn
(Anna, don't cry)
We've still got something to pawn.

Glory's back in the air
(Anna, don't cry)
I've looked in the larder; there's nothing there.

They say there'll be victories yet
(Anna, don't cry)
Here's one they're not going to get.

We've launched the attack
(Anna, don't cry)
If I do come back
It's other colours I'll be coming under.

EPITAPH FOR GORKI

Here lies
The ambassador of the slums
The man who described the tormentors of the people
And those who fought the tormentors
Who was educated in the universities of the highways
The man of low birth who helped to do away with
The system of high and low
The people's teacher
Who learned from the people.

THOUGHT IN THE WORKS OF THE CLASSICS

Naked and undraped
It comes before you, without shame, for it is

Certain of its usefulness.
It is not distressed
That you know it already, all it asks is
That you should have forgotten it.
It speaks
With the arrogance of greatness. Without ceremony
Without introduction
It enters, accustomed
To find respect because it is useful.
Its audience is misery, which is timeless.
Cold and hunger keep close watch
On the audience's attention. The least inattention
Condemns them to immediate ruin.
But however masterfully it enters
It yet shows that it is nothing without its audience
Would neither have come nor know
Where to go or where to stay
If they do not take it in. Indeed, uninstructed by them
Who were still ignorant yesterday
It would fast lose its strength and hastily degenerate.

THE DOUBTER

Whenever we seemed
To have found the answer to a question
One of us untied the string of the old rolled-up
Chinese scroll on the wall, so that it fell down and
Revealed to us the man on the bench who
Doubted so much.

I, he said to us
Am the doubter. I am doubtful whether
The work was well done that devoured your days.
Whether what you said would still have value for anyone if it
        were less well said.
Whether you said it well but perhaps

Were not convinced of the truth of what you said.
Whether it is not ambiguous; each possible misunderstanding
Is your responsibility. Or it can be unambiguous
And take the contradictions out of things; is it too
      unambiguous?
If so, what you say is useless. Your thing has no life in it.
Are you truly in the stream of happening? Do you accept
All that develops? Are *you* developing? Who are you? To
      whom
Do you speak? Who finds what you say useful? And, by the
      way:
Is it sobering? Can it be read in the morning?
Is it also linked to what is already there? Are the sentences
      that were
Spoken before you made use of, or at least refuted? Is
      everything verifiable?
By experience? By which one? But above all
Always above all else: how does one act
If one believes what you say? Above all: how does one act?

Reflectively, curiously, we studied the doubting
Blue man on the scroll, looked at each other and
Made a fresh start.

NATURE POEMS

I (*Svendborg*)

Through the window, those twelve squares
I see a gnarled pear tree with hanging branches
On an uneven lawn on which some straw lies.
It is bordered by a tract of dug soil
In which bushes have been planted, and low trees.
Behind that hedge, bare now in winter
Runs the footpath, bordered by a fence
Of knee-high slats, painted white: three feet behind it

A little house with two windows in green wooden frames
And a tiled roof as high as the wall.
The wall is freshly whitewashed, and the yard or two of wall
That continues the house to one side, built on later
Is also freshly whitewashed. As on the left, where it recedes a
     little
There is a green wooden door in the extension too
And since on the other side of the house the Sound begins
Whose surface is covered in mist towards the right
Wooden shed and shrubs in front of it
The little house, I suppose, has three exits in all.
That is good for tenants who oppose injustice
And could be called for by the police.

II (*Augsburg*)

A spring evening in the outskirts.
The four houses of the estate
Look white in the dusk.
The workmen are still sitting
At the dark tables in the yard.
They talk of the yellow peril.
A few little girls go for beer
Although the brass bell of the Ursuline convent has already
     rung.
In shirtsleeves their fathers lean over the window sills.
Their neighbours wrap the peach trees on the house wall
In little white rags against the night frost.

EVERY YEAR IN SEPTEMBER

Every year in September when the school term begins
The women stand in the stationers' on the city's outskirts
And buy textbooks and exercise books for their children.
Desperately they fish out their last pennies

From their tattered handbags, moaning
That knowledge costs so much. They have no inkling
How bad the knowledge is that is prescribed
For their children.

OUR POORER SCHOOLFELLOWS FROM THE CITY'S OUTSKIRTS

Our poorer schoolfellows in their thin overcoats
Always came too late for the morning period
Because they had been delivering milk or newspapers for their
      mothers.
The teachers
Put them in the black book and told them off.

They brought no sandwiches. During break they
Wrote up their homework in the bogs.
That was not allowed. The break
Was meant for recreation and for eating.

When they did not know the decimal value of π
Their teachers asked them: why
Did you not stay in the gutter you came from?
But that they did know.

The poorer schoolchildren from the city's outskirts were
      promised
Minor posts in government service.
So they learned the contents of their
Tattered second-hand books by heart in the sweat of their
      brow
Learned to lick the teachers' boots and
Despise their own mothers.

Those minor posts for the poorer schoolchildren from the
      city's outskirts
Lay under the sod. Their office chairs had

No seats. Their outlook
Consisted of the roots of short plants. To what end were they
Made to learn Greek grammar and Caesar's campaigns
The formula for sulphur and the value of π?
In the mass graves of Flanders, for which they were destined
What need had they of anything but
A little quicklime?

TRAVELLING IN A COMFORTABLE CAR

Travelling in a comfortable car
Down a rainy road in the country
We saw a ragged fellow at nightfall
Signal to us for a ride, with a low bow.
We had a roof and we had room and we drove on
And we heard me say, in a grumpy voice: no
We can't take anyone with us.
We had gone on a long way, perhaps a day's march
When suddenly I was shocked by this voice of mine
This behaviour of mine and this
Whole world.

IN DARK TIMES

They won't say: when the walnut tree shook in the wind
But: when the house-painter crushed the workers.
They won't say: when the child skimmed a flat stone across
      the rapids
But: when the great wars were being prepared for.
They won't say: when the woman came into the room
But: when the great powers joined forces against the workers.
However, they won't say: the times were dark
Rather: why were their poets silent?

THE LEAVETAKING

We embrace each other.
My hands touch the rich material
Yours touch the shoddy.
The embrace is hasty
You are on your way to a good meal
The executioner's men
Are after me.
We speak of the weather and of our
Enduring friendship. Anything else
Would be too bitter.

THE NINETEENTH SONNET

One day when no communication came
I called the guardians, the six elephants
To the Triumphal Arch and saw them stand
At midnight in the Avenue Wagram.

They eyed me, gently swaying, as I said:
'When first I handed her into your care
I told you all who gave offence to her
Should seven times be stamped on till they're dead.'

They stood in silence till the biggest one
Lifting his trunk to trumpet spitefully
Aimed slowly at the guilty party: me.

And thundering the herd advanced. I ran –
Ran, while they followed, to the Post to write
A letter, glancing through the door in fright.

THE ABSTEMIOUS CHANCELLOR

They tell me the chancellor doesn't drink
Eats no meat and never smokes
And he lives in a modest dwelling.
But they also tell me the poor
Starve and die in misery.
How much better it would be to have a state of which men
     said:
The chancellor is always drunk at cabinet meetings
Eyeing the smoke from their pipes, a few
Uneducated men sit altering the laws
There are no poor.

ON VIOLENCE

The headlong stream is termed violent
But the river bed hemming it in is
Termed violent by no one.

The storm that bends the birch trees
Is held to be violent
But how about the storm
That bends the backs of the roadworkers?

ON STERILITY

The fruit tree that bears no fruit
Is called sterile. Who
Examines the soil?

The branch that breaks
Is called rotten, but
Wasn't there snow on it?

QUOTATION

The poet Kin said:
How am I to write immortal works if I am not famous?
How am I to answer if I am not asked?
Why should I waste time on verses if they will waste away
        with time?
I write my suggestions in a durable language
Since I fear it will be some time till they are carried out.
To achieve a great goal, great changes are required.
Little changes are the enemies of great changes.
I have enemies. Therefore I must be famous.

THE GOOD COMRADE M.S.

I came to you all as a teacher, and as a teacher
I could have left you. As I was learning however
I stayed. For even after that
Fleeing for shelter beneath the Danish thatch
I did not leave you.
And you gave me one of you
To go with me.

So that she could examine
All I said; so that she could improve
Every line from then on.
Schooled in the school of fighters
Against oppression.

Since then she has been my support –
In poor health but
High spirits, not to be suborned
Even by me. Many a time
I cross out a line myself, laughing as I imagine
What she would say about it.

Against others however she defends me.
I have heard that when she was ill she rose from her bed
To explain to you the use of the didactic plays
Because she knows I am striving
To serve your cause.

Five Songs of the Soldier of the Revolution

SONG OF THE SOLDIER OF THE
REVOLUTION

1

I, the soldier of the Revolution, know
It makes no difference where I go.
Any room will do as somewhere to live.
However dirty or dark, I'll make shift
To make it a strongpoint where I can put
My gun in position ready to shoot.

2

I don't care a bit what the area is like
I can see at once what the people lack.
The average area's not so bad
Only that lot who think they know how to lead.
That lot has got to be met fair and square
Then life will be bearable everywhere.

3

I don't need friendship either, since
I always report to my unit at once.
Those are my friends, those men standing there
Though I may never have seen them before.
I'd know them as friends by day or night
Because they stand by me ready to fight.

4

My friends will go out and fetch me bread
They'll din the new passwords into my head
They'll bind up my wounds and relieve my pain
And guide me back to the hole in the wall again
So I can return to the place once more
Which I had to abandon just before.

5

And supposing I can't limp back that far
I'll go on fighting wherever we are
By looking around me and trying to find out
Just what makes a victory and what makes a rout.
In that sense there are battle positions untold
Which a soldier of the Revolution can hold.

LUCK OF THE SOLDIER OF THE REVOLUTION

The soldier is in luck.
The ships that carry him
Sail well and win esteem
And bring him safely back.

His rifle is good too.
The best you can get here.
It deserves to be held so dear
And cared for as is due.

His unit is firm as steel
And far and wide it's known
For doing all that can be done
With understanding and skill.

The soldier is in luck.
When the battle's at its height
Courage lends him strength to fight
And he will not turn back.

STANDING ORDERS FOR THE SOLDIER M.S.

1

Say what you like
About life, it's a mess.

Time for a break:
Let's hear what the soldier says.
   I'll give it you from the shoulder:
   Don't muck about with me.
   I am a soldier
   So you'd better let it be.

2

The country where I tread
(It could be a room instead)
Is conquered and occupied
And I'm in charge as from now
And it's certainly not just for show.
And resistance will be swept aside.
   Room, this is straight from the shoulder:
   Don't muck about with me.
   I am a soldier
   So you'd better let it be.

3

I treat my equipment with care
My tunic that cannot tear
My rifle that I call Clare
My military flair
All laid out neatly there.
   Brother, this is straight from the shoulder:
   Don't muck about with me.
   I am a soldier
   So you'd better let it be.

4

The soldier keeps this in mind
And tries to take it to heart:
When the difficulty
Of the mountains is once behind
That's when you'll see
The difficulty of the plains will start.

Difficulty, this is straight from the shoulder:
Don't muck about with me.
I am a soldier
So you'd better let it be.

5

The soldier gives orders for victory.
He refuses to lie around the scenery.
But so long as the orders come all is well.
The soldier will always find a hole.
World, this is straight from the shoulder:
Don't muck about with me.
I am a soldier
So you'd better let it be.

6

The soldier marches (he may limp on occasion)
He's not beaten until he dies.
The place where he lies
Is under occupation.
Place, this is straight from the shoulder:
Don't muck about with me.
I am a soldier
So you'd better let it be.

THE SOLDIER OF THE REVOLUTION
MOCKED AT

General with the leaky boots
Those orders you obey:
Can you tell me whose they are? And:
Have you had a meal today?

So you've got big plans in your head?
Except: your stomach is empty.
You say you have a flag
But where is your army?

Statesman with the one pair of trousers
Do you have an ironing board in your command?
Or is it beneath the bridge that
Your cabinet is summoned?

The king takes the knave
The ace takes the king.
Your name will go down in history
But your personal papers are lacking.

If two and two make four
Then you'll get power all right
(Top will be bottom then) but:
Have you got a bed for tonight?

HIS REPLY

If I'm to wear boots that keep out the wet
For these ones don't cover my feet
Then I must kick out all who regret
They have no boots for me each time we meet –
Must have the whole leather market.

My trousers are falling apart.
To endure the winter even a bit
I need trousers round where I sit
So I must know where the trousers have gone, for a start –
Must have the whole textile industry in my pocket.

If I want bread that's fit to eat
I must break up the wheat exchanges first
And go out and win the farmers' trust
And send machines into the fields to harvest the wheat –
Must farm on an enormous scale, that's what.

As for those who held me down in the past
And whose wars I'm not prepared to fight
I must laugh at whatever they say or write
And nail my flag (a red one) to the mast
And declare my own war on the lot.

RANGED IN THE WELL-TRIED SYSTEM

Ranged in the well-tried system of my relationships
(An elastic network) I have long avoided
New encounters. Keenly concerned not to test
My friends by imposing on them
And not to allot specific
Functions to them
I restrict myself to the possible.
So long as I keep from falling
I shall not expect the impossible to be provided
So long as I do not grow weak
I shall not encounter weakness.
But the new people may
Be appreciated by others.

BEGINNING OF THE WAR

Once Germany has been armed to the teeth
She will suffer a grievous wrong
And the drummer will wage his war.

You, though, will defend Germany
In foreign countries, unknown to you
And fight against people like yourselves.

The drummer will drool about liberation
But the oppression within the country will be unparalleled.

And he may manage to win every battle
Except the last one.

Once the drummer's war is lost
Germany's war will be won.

From a German War Primer

AMONGST THE HIGHLY PLACED
It is considered low to talk about food.
The fact is: they have
Already eaten.

The lowly must leave this earth
Without having tasted
Any good meat.

For wondering where they come from and
Where they are going
The fine evenings find them
Too exhausted.

They have not yet seen
The mountains and the great sea
When their time is already up.

If the lowly do not
Think about what's low
They will never rise.

THE BREAD OF THE HUNGRY HAS
ALL BEEN EATEN
Meat has become unknown. Useless
The pouring out of the people's sweat.
The laurel groves have been
Lopped down.
From the chimneys of the arms factories
Rises smoke.

THE HOUSE-PAINTER SPEAKS OF
GREAT TIMES TO COME
The forests still grow.
The fields still bear
The cities still stand.
The people still breathe.

ON THE CALENDAR THE DAY IS NOT
YET SHOWN
Every month, every day
Lies open still. One of those days
Is going to be marked with a cross.

THE WORKERS CRY OUT FOR BREAD
The merchants cry out for markets.
The unemployed were hungry. The employed
Are hungry now.
The hands that lay folded are busy again.
They are making shells.

THOSE WHO TAKE THE MEAT FROM THE TABLE
Teach contentment.
Those for whom the contribution is destined
Demand sacrifice.
Those who eat their fill speak to the hungry
Of wonderful times to come.
Those who lead the country into the abyss
Call ruling too difficult
For ordinary men.

WHEN THE LEADERS SPEAK OF PEACE
The common folk know
That war is coming.

When the leaders curse war
The mobilisation order is already written out.

THOSE AT THE TOP SAY: PEACE
AND WAR
Are of different substance.
But their peace and their war
Are like wind and storm.

War grows from their peace
Like son from his mother
He bears
Her frightful features.

Their war kills
Whatever their peace
Has left over.

ON THE WALL WAS CHALKED:
They want war.
The man who wrote it
Has already fallen.

THOSE AT THE TOP SAY:
This way to glory.
Those down below say:
This way to the grave.

THE WAR WHICH IS COMING
Is not the first one. There were
Other wars before it.
When the last one came to an end
There were conquerors and conquered.
Among the conquered the common people
Starved. Among the conquerors
The common people starved too.

THOSE AT THE TOP SAY COMRADESHIP
Reigns in the army.
The truth of this is seen

In the cookhouse.
In their hearts should be
The selfsame courage. But
On their plates
Are two kinds of rations.

WHEN IT COMES TO MARCHING MANY DO NOT
KNOW
That their enemy is marching at their head.
The voice which gives them their orders
Is their enemy's voice and
The man who speaks of the enemy
Is the enemy himself.

IT IS NIGHT
The married couples
Lie in their beds. The young women
Will bear orphans.

GENERAL, YOUR TANK IS A POWERFUL VEHICLE
It smashes down forests and crushes a hundred men.
But it has one defect:
It needs a driver.

General, your bomber is powerful.
It flies faster than a storm and carries more than an elephant.
But it has one defect:
It needs a mechanic.

General, man is very useful.
He can fly and he can kill.
But he has one defect:
He can think.

WASHING
C.N.

When years ago I showed you
How to wash first thing in the morning
With bits of ice in the water
Of the little copper bowl
Immersing your face, your eyes open
Then, while you dried yourself with the rough towel
Reading the difficult lines of your part
From the sheet pinned to the wall, I said:
That's something you're doing for yourself; make it
Exemplary.

Now I hear that you are said to be in prison.
The letters I wrote on your behalf
Remained unanswered. The friends I approached for you
Are silent. I can do nothing for you. What
Will your morning bring? Will you still do something for
        yourself?
Hopeful and responsible
With good movements, exemplary?

THE BUDDHA'S PARABLE OF THE BURNING HOUSE

Gautama the Buddha taught
The doctrine of greed's wheel to which we are bound, and
        advised
That we should shed all craving and thus
Undesiring enter the nothingness that he called Nirvana.
Then one day his pupils asked him:
What is it like, this nothingness, Master? Every one of us
        would
Shed all craving, as you advise, but tell us
Whether this nothingness which then we shall enter
Is perhaps like being at one with all creation

When you lie in water, your body weightless, at noon
Unthinking almost, lazily lie in the water, or drowse
Hardly knowing now that you straighten the blanket
Going down fast – whether this nothingness, then
Is a happy one of this kind, a pleasant nothingness, or
Whether this nothing of yours is mere nothing, cold, senseless
    and void.
Long the Buddha was silent, then said nonchalantly:
There is no answer to your question.
But in the evening, when they had gone
The Buddha still sat under the bread-fruit tree, and to the
    others
To those who had not asked, addressed this parable:
Lately I saw a house. It was burning. The flame
Licked at its roof. I went up close and observed
That there were people still inside. I opened the door and
    called
Out to them that the roof was ablaze, so exhorting them
To leave at once. But those people
Seemed in no hurry. One of them
When the heat was already scorching his eyebrows
Asked me what it was like outside, whether it wasn't raining
Whether the wind wasn't blowing perhaps, whether there
    was
Another house for them, and more of this kind. Without
    answering
I went out again. These people here, I thought
Need to burn to death before they stop asking questions.
    Truly, friends
Unless a man feels the ground so hot underfoot that he'd
    gladly
Exchange it for any other, sooner than stay, to him
I have nothing to say. Thus Gautama the Buddha.
But we too, no longer concerned with the art of submission
Rather with that of not submitting, and putting forward
Various proposals of an earthly nature, and beseeching men
    to shake off

Their human tormentors, we too believe that to those
Who in face of the approaching bomber squadrons of Capital
        go on asking too long
How we propose to do this, and how we envisage that
And what will become of their savings and Sunday trousers
        after a revolution
We have nothing much to say.

A WORKER'S SPEECH TO A DOCTOR

We know what makes us ill.
When we are ill we are told
That it's you who will heal us.

For ten years, we are told
You learned healing in fine schools
Built at the people's expense
And to get your knowledge
Spent a fortune.
So you must be able to heal.

Are you able to heal?

When we come to you
Our rags are torn off us
And you listen all over our naked body.
As to the cause of our illness
One glance at our rags would
Tell you more. It is the same cause that wears out
Our bodies and our clothes.

The pain in our shoulder comes
You say, from the damp; and this is also the reason
For the stain on the wall of our flat.
So tell us:
Where does the damp come from?

Too much work and too little food
Make us feeble and thin.
Your prescription says:
Put on more weight.
You might as well tell a bullrush
Not to get wet.

How much time can you give us?
We see: one carpet in your flat costs
The fees you earn from
Five thousand consultations.

You'll no doubt say
You are innocent. The damp patch
On the wall of our flats
Tells the same story.

German Satires

When the Regime commanded that books with harmful
    knowledge
Should be publicly burned and on all sides
Oxen were forced to drag cartloads of books
To the bonfires, a banished
Writer, one of the best, scanning the list of the
Burned, was shocked to find that his
Books had been passed over. He rushed to his desk
On wings of wrath, and wrote a letter to those in power
Burn me! he wrote with flying pen, burn me! Haven't my
    books
Always reported the truth? And here you are
Treating me like a liar! I command you:
Burn me!

DREAM ABOUT A GREAT GRUMBLER
(DURING A POTATO SHORTAGE)

I had a dream:
Opposite the opera house
Where the house-painter had gone to make his big speech
Suddenly a colossal potato, bigger than an average hill, lay
Before the expectant people, and
Also made a speech.
I, he said in a deep voice
Have come to warn you. Of course I know
I'm only a potato, a small
Unimportant person, not noticed much, hardly mentioned
In the history books, without influence
In top society. When there's talk of great things

Of 'honour' and 'glory', I take a back seat.
It's said to be ignoble
To put me before glory. Yet I've done my bit
To help people go on living in this vale of tears.
Now the time has come to choose
Between me and that man in there. Now
It's him or me. If you choose him
You lose me. But if you should need me
You must throw him out. And so I think
You shouldn't spend too long in there, listening to that man
Who'll throw me out neck and crop. Even if he says you'll die
If you rebel against him, you must bear in mind
That without me you'll die too, and so will your children.

Thus spake the potato, and slowly
As the house-painter went on bellowing in the opera house
Audible to the entire people through the loudspeakers, he
      began, as if to show what he meant
To stage a weird demonstration, visible to the entire people,
      shrinking
With every word the house-painter uttered
Getting smaller, shabbier, and seedier.

DIFFICULTY OF GOVERNING

1
Ministers are always telling the people
How difficult it is to govern. Without the ministers
Corn would grow into the ground, not upward.
Not a lump of coal would leave the mine if
The Chancellor weren't so clever. Without the Minister of
      Propaganda
No girl would ever agree to get pregnant. Without the
      Minister of War
There'd never be a war. Indeed, whether the sun would rise
      in the morning

Without the Führer's permission
Is very doubtful, and if it did, it would be
In the wrong place.

2
It's just as difficult, so they tell us
To run a factory. Without the owner
The walls would fall in and the machines rust, so they say.
Even if a plough could get made somewhere
It would never reach a field without the
Cunning words the factory owner writes the peasants: who
Could otherwise tell them that ploughs exist? And what
Would become of an estate without the landlord? Surely
They'd be sowing rye where they had set the potatoes.

3
If governing were easy
There'd be no need for such inspired minds as the Führer's.
If the worker knew how to run his machine and
The peasant could tell his field from a pastryboard
There'd be no need of factory owner or landlord.
It's only because they are all so stupid
That a few are needed who are so clever.

4
Or could it be that
Governing is so difficult only
Because swindling and exploitation take some learning?

THE ANXIETIES OF THE REGIME

1
A foreigner, returning from a trip to the Third Reich
When asked who really ruled there, answered:
Fear.

2

Anxiously
The scholar breaks off his discussion to inspect
The thin partitions of his study, his face ashen. The teacher
Lies sleepless, worrying over
An ambiguous phrase the inspector had let fall.
The old woman in the grocer's shop
Puts her trembling finger to her lips to hold back
Her angry exclamation about the bad flour. Anxiously
The doctor inspects the strangulation marks on his patient's
                 throat.
Full of anxiety, parents look at their children as at traitors.
Even the dying
Hush their failing voices as they
Take leave of their relatives.

3

But likewise the brownshirts themselves
Fear the man whose arm doesn't fly up
And are terrified of the man who
Wishes them a good morning.
The shrill voices of those who give orders
Are full of fear like the squeaking of
Piglets awaiting the butcher's knife, as their fat arses
Sweat with anxiety in their office chairs.
Driven by anxiety
They break into homes and search the lavatories
And it is anxiety
That makes them burn whole libraries. Thus
Fear rules not only those who are ruled, but
The rulers too.

4

Why do they so fear the open word?

5

Given the immense power of the regime
Its camps and torture cellars

Its well-fed policemen
Its intimidated or corrupt judges
Its card indexes and lists of suspected persons
Which fill whole buildings to the roof
One would think they wouldn't have to
Fear an open word from a simple man.

6
But their Third Reich recalls
The house of Tar, the Assyrian, that mighty fortress
Which, according to the legend, could not be taken by any
        army, but
When one single, distinct word was spoken inside it
Fell to dust.

WORDS THE LEADER CANNOT BEAR TO HEAR

In the ministries it is well known that the Leader winces
Whenever he hears words which begin with the syllable PRO –
Such words as 'proletarian', 'prose', 'provocation' or 'pro
        and con'.
'Prostitution' and 'profit' seem to disquiet him too.
Whenever these words are mentioned in his presence
He glances up shyly with a hunted, guilty expression
Which the speaker is hard put to explain.
Another syllable which causes him difficulty
Is the syllable GRAM, occurring in the word 'gramme'
Which designates a small unit of weight, and in words such
        as 'grammar'. Since the Leader
Exhibits such antipathy toward these two syllables, it follows
Quite naturally that, above all, a word which contains them
        both
May never under any circumstances be uttered in his presence –
Wherefore, at Party and theatrical functions
The word PROGRAMME is always replaced by the expression
        'sequence of events'.

PROHIBITION OF THEATRE CRITICISM

When the Minister of Propaganda
Wanted to forbid criticism of the government by the people
      he
Forbade theatre criticism. The regime
Dearly loves the theatre. Its accomplishments
Are mainly on the theatrical plane.
Its brilliant manipulation of the spotlight
Has done no less for it than has its
Brilliant manipulation of the rubber truncheon.
Its gala performances
Are broadcast by radio across the entire Reich.
In three supercolossal films
Of which the last was 26,000 feet long
The leading actor played the Führer.
So as to develop the people's feeling for the theatre
Visits to these performances are arranged on a compulsory
      basis.
Each year on the First of May
When the Reich's first actor
Appears in the role of a former worker
Spectators are actually paid to attend: two marks
A head. No expense is spared for the Festival
Which takes place near Bayreuth under the name REICHS-
      PARTEITAG.
The Chancellor himself
Appears as a Parsifal-like simpleton singing
Twice daily his famous aria
NIE SOLLST DU MICH BEFRAGEN.
It is clear that such expensive productions
Need shielding from any breath of criticism.
What might not result
If one and all could criticise
Reich Youth Leader Baldur's undue use of make-up
Or the fact that the Propaganda Minister's voice rings so
      false that

One cannot believe a single thing about him, not even
His club foot? In short all this theatre calls for
A complete ban on the voicing of criticism; in fact it must
Not even be said what the play is
Who is paying for the performance and
Who acts the chief part.

GUNS BEFORE BUTTER

1

The famous remark of General Goering
That guns should come before butter
Is correct inasmuch as the government needs
The more guns the less butter it has
For the less butter it has
The more enemies.

2

Furthermore it should be said that
Guns on an empty stomach
Are not to every people's taste.
Merely swallowing gas
They say, does not quench thirst
And without woollen pants
A soldier, it could be, is brave only in summer.

3

When the artillery runs out of ammunition
Officers up front tend
To get holes in their backs.

CONCERNING THE LABEL EMIGRANT

I always found the name false which they gave us: Emigrants.
That means those who leave their country. But we
Did not leave, of our own free will
Choosing another land. Nor did we enter
Into a land, to stay there, if possible for ever.
Merely, we fled. We are driven out, banned.
Not a home, but an exile, shall the land be that took us in.
Restlessly we wait thus, as near as we can to the frontier
Awaiting the day of return, every smallest alteration
Observing beyond the boundary, zealously asking
Every arrival, forgetting nothing and giving up nothing
And also not forgiving anything which happened, forgiving
        nothing.
Ah, the silence of the Sound does not deceive us! We hear
        the shrieks
From their camps even here. Yes, we ourselves
Are almost like rumours of crimes, which escaped
Over the frontier. Every one of us
Who with torn shoes walks through the crowd
Bears witness to the shame which now defiles our land.
But none of us
Will stay here. The final word
Is yet unspoken.

THOUGHTS ON THE DURATION OF EXILE

I
Don't knock any nails in the wall
Just throw your coat on the chair.
Why plan for four days?
Tomorrow you'll go back home.

Leave the little tree without water.
Why plant a tree now?
You'll pack your bags and be away
Before it's as high as a doorstep.

Pull your cap over your eyes when people pass.
What use thumbing through a foreign grammar?
The message that calls you home
Is written in a language you know.

As whitewash peels from the ceiling
(Do nothing to stop it!)
So the block of force will crumble
That has been set up at the frontier
To keep out justice.

II
Look at the nail you knocked into the wall:
When do you think you will go back?
Do you want to know what your heart of hearts is saying?
Day after day
You work for the liberation.
You sit in your room, writing.
Do you want to know what you think of your work?
Look at the little chestnut tree in the corner of the yard –
You carried a full can of water to it.

PLACE OF REFUGE

An oar lies on the roof. A moderate wind
Will not carry away the thatch.
In the yard posts are set for
The children's swing.

The mail comes twice a day
Where letters would be welcome.
Down the Sound come the ferries.
The house has four doors to escape by.

SPRING 1938

I

To-day, Easter Sunday morning
A sudden snowstorm swept over the island.
Between the greening hedges lay snow. My young son
Drew me to a little apricot tree by the house wall
Away from a verse in which I pointed the finger at those
Who were preparing a war which
Could well wipe out the continent, this island, my people, my
        family
And myself. In silence
We put a sack
Over the freezing tree.

II

Above the Sound hang rainclouds, but the garden is
Gilded still by the sun. The pear trees
Have green leaves and no blossom yet, the cherries
Blossom and no leaves yet. The white clusters
Seem to sprout from withered branches.
Across the wrinkled waters of the sound
Goes a little boat with a patched sail.
The starlings' twittering
Is broken by the distant thunder
Of naval gunfire from the war games
Of the Third Reich.

III
In the willows by the Sound
These spring nights the screech-owl often calls.
According to a peasant superstition
Your screech-owl informs people that
They haven't long to live. I
Who know full well that I have told the truth
About the powers that be, don't need a death-bird
To inform me so.

THE CHERRY THIEF

Early one morning, long before cockcrow
I was wakened by whistling and went to the window.
In my cherry tree – grey dawn filled the garden –
Sat a young man, with patched up trousers
Cheerfully picking my cherries. Seeing me
He nodded, and with both hands
Pulled the cherries from the branches into his pockets.
For quite a while as I lay once more in bed
I heard him whistling his gay little song.

REPORT ON A CASTAWAY

When the castaway set foot on our island
He came like one who has reached his goal.
I almost believe that when he sighted us
Who had run up to help him
He at once felt pity for us.
From the very beginning
He concerned himself with our affairs only.
Using the lessons of his shipwreck
He taught us to sail. Courage even
He instilled in us. Of the stormy waters
He spoke with great respect, doubtless

Because they had defeated a man like him. In doing so
They had of course revealed many of their tricks. This
Knowledge, he said, would make us, his pupils
Better men. Since he missed certain dishes
He improved our cooking.
Though visibly dissatisfied with himself
He was not for a moment satisfied with the state of affairs
Surrounding himself and us. But never
In all the time he spent with us
Did we hear him complain of anyone but himself.
He died of an old wound. Even as he lay on his back he
Was testing a new knot for our fishing nets. Thus
He died learning.

ON THE DEATH OF A FIGHTER FOR PEACE

In memoriam Carl von Ossietzky

He who would not give in
Has been done to death
He who was done to death
Would not give in.

The warner's mouth
Is stopped with earth.
The bloody adventure
Begins.
Over the grave of one who loved peace
Slog the battalions.

Was the fight in vain, then?

When he who did not fight alone is done to death
The enemy
Has not yet won.

EMIGRANT'S LAMENT

I earned my bread and ate it just like you.
I am a doctor; or at least I was.
The colour of my hair, shape of my nose
Cost me my home, my bread and butter too.

She who for seven years had slept with me
My hand upon her lap, her face against my face
Took me to court. The cause of my disgrace:
My hair was black. So she got rid of me.

But I escaped at night-time through a wood
(For reasons of my mother's ancestry)
To find a country that would be my host.

Yet when I asked for work it was no good.
You are impertinent, they said to me.
I'm not impertinent, I said: I'm lost.

Four Theatre Poems

PORTRAYAL OF PAST AND PRESENT IN ONE

Whatever you portray you should always portray
As if it were happening now. Engrossed
The silent crowd sits in the darkness, lured
Away from its routine affairs. Now
The fisherman's wife is being brought her son whom
The generals have killed. Even what has just happened
In her room is wiped out. What is happening here is
Happening now and just the once. To act in this way
Is habitual with you, and now I am advising you
To ally this habit with yet another: that is, that your acting
    should
At the same time express the fact that this instant
On your stage is often repeated; only yesterday
You were acting it, and tomorrow too
Given spectators, there will be a further performance.
Nor should you let the Now blot out the
Previously and Afterwards, nor for that matter whatever
Is even now happening outside the theatre and is similar in
    kind
Nor even things that have nothing to do with it all – none of
    this
Should you allow to be entirely forgotten.
So you should simply make the instant
Stand out, without in the process hiding
What you are making it stand out from. Give your acting
That progression of one-thing-after-another, that attitude of
Working up what you have taken on. In this way
You will show the flow of events and also the course
Of your work, permitting the spectator
To experience this Now on many levels, coming from
    Previously and

Merging into Afterwards, also having much else now
Alongside it. He is sitting not only
In your theatre but also
In the world.

ON JUDGING

You artists who, for pleasure or for pain
Deliver yourselves up to the judgement of the audience
Be moved in future
To deliver up also to the judgement of the audience
The world which you show.

You should show what is; but also
In showing what is you should suggest what could be and
    is not
And might be helpful. For from your portrayal
The audience must learn to deal with what is portrayed.
Let this learning be pleasurable. Learning must be taught
As an art, and you should
Teach dealing with things and with people
As an art too, and the practice of art is pleasurable.

To be sure, you live in a dark time. You see man
Tossed back and forth like a ball by evil forces.
Only an idiot lives without worry. The unsuspecting
Are already destined to go under. What were the earthquakes
Of grey prehistory compared to the afflictions
Which we suffer in cities? What were bad harvests
To the need that ravages us in the midst of plenty?

ON THE CRITICAL ATTITUDE

The critical attitude
Strikes many people as unfruitful.

That is because they find the state
Impervious to their criticism.
But what in this case is an unfruitful attitude
Is merely a feeble attitude. Give criticism arms
And states can be demolished by it.

Canalising a river
Grafting a fruit tree
Educating a person
Transforming a state
These are instances of fruitful criticism
And at the same time
Instances of art.

THEATRE OF EMOTIONS

Between ourselves, it seems to me a sorry trade
Putting on plays solely
To stir up inert feelings. You remind me of masseurs
Sinking their fingers in all too fatty
Flanks, as in dough, to knead away sluggards'
Bellies. Your situations are hastily assembled to
Excite the customers to rage
Or pain. The audience
Thus become voyeurs. The sated
Sit next the hungry.

The emotions you manufacture are turbid and impure
General and blurred, no less false
Than thoughts can be. Dull blows on the backbone
Cause the dregs of the soul to rise to the surface.
With glassy eyes
Sweaty brow and tightened calves
The poisoned audience follows
Your exhibitions.

No wonder they buy their tickets
Two by two. And no wonder
They like to sit in the dark that hides them.

Literary Sonnets

ON SHAKESPEARE'S PLAY *HAMLET*

Here is the body, puffy and inert
Where we can trace the virus of the mind.
How lost he seems among his steel-clad kind
This introspective sponger in a shirt.

Till they bring drums to wake him up again
As Fortinbras and all the fools he's found
March off to battle for that patch of ground
'Which is not tomb enough . . . to hide the slain'.

At that his too, too solid flesh sees red.
He feels he's hesitated long enough.
It's time to turn to (bloody) deeds instead.

So we nod grimly when the play is done
And they pronounce that he was of the stuff
To prove 'most royally', 'had he been put on'.

ON LENZ'S BOURGEOIS TRAGEDY *THE TUTOR*

Here you've a trans-Rhenanian Figaro!
The nobles get their schooling with the crowd
Which that side won the fight, and this side bowed:
So there it made a comedy, and here not so.

Poor man, his eyes seek his rich pupil's blouse
And not the literature they're meant to read.
He ought to cut the Gordian knot. Instead
All he can do, the lackey, is cut loose.

His bread and butter, he soon recognises
Lift out of reach each time his member rises.
He's got to choose, then; and he makes his choice.

His gut may rumble, but he knows his station.
He cries, groans, curses, opts for self-castration.
Describing it, tears break the poet's voice.

ON KANT'S DEFINITION OF MARRIAGE IN *THE METAPHYSIC OF ETHICS*

That pact for reciprocity in use
Of sexual organs and worldly possessions
Which marriage meant for him, in my submission
Urgently needs securing from abuse.

I gather certain partners have defaulted.
Allegedly the organs acting for them
Vanished when they decided to withdraw them.
Loopholes were found: something that must be halted.

Recourse to law would seem the only way
To get those organs duly confiscated.
Maybe the partners ought to be persuaded

To check again on what the contracts say.
If they won't do so, someone's sure to send
The bailiffs in – a most unhappy end.

ON THE DECAY OF LOVE

Your mothers gave birth with pain, but your women
Conceive with pain.

The act of love
Shall no longer prosper. Breeding still happens, but
The embrace is an embrace of wrestlers. The women
Have raised their arms in defence while
They are held by their possessors.

The rustic milkmaid, famous
For her capacity to feel joy in
The embrace, looks up with contempt at
Her unhappy sisters in sables
Who are paid for every wriggle of their pampered bottoms.

The patient spring
Which has slaked the thirst of so many generations
Sees with horror how the last of them
Gulps the draught from it, sour-visaged.

Every animal can do it. Among these people
It's considered an art.

THE PEASANT'S ADDRESS TO HIS OX
(after an Egyptian peasant's song of 1400 B.C.)

O ox, our godly puller of the plough
Please humour us by pulling straight, and kindly
Do not get the furrows crossed.
Lead the way, o leader, gee-up!
We stooped for days on end to harvest your fodder.
Allow yourself to try just a little, dearest provider.
While you are eating, do not fret about the furrows: eat!
For your stall, o protector of the family

We carried the tons of timber by hand. We
Sleep in the damp, you in the dry. Yesterday
You had a cough, beloved pacemaker.
We were beside ourselves. You won't
Peg out before the sowing, will you, you dog?

LEGEND OF THE ORIGIN OF THE BOOK
TAO-TÊ-CHING ON LAO-TSÛ'S ROAD INTO EXILE

1

Once he was seventy and getting brittle
Quiet retirement seemed the teacher's due.
In his country goodness had been weakening a little
And the wickedness was gaining ground anew.
So he buckled on his shoe.

2

And he packed up what he would be needing:
Not much. But enough to travel light.
Items like the book that he was always reading
And the pipe he used to smoke at night.
Bread as much as he thought right.

3

Gladly looked back at his valley, then forgot it
As he turned to take the mountain track.
And the ox was glad of the fresh grass it spotted
Munching, with the old man on its back
Happy that the pace was slack.

4

Four days out among the rocks, a barrier
Where a customs man made them report.
'What valuables have you to declare here?'
And the boy leading the ox explained: 'The old man taught'.
Nothing at all, in short.

5

Then the man, in cheerful disposition
Asked again: 'How did he make out, pray?'
Said the boy: 'He learnt how quite soft water, by attrition
Over the years will grind strong rocks away.
In other words, that hardness must lose the day.'

6

Then the boy tugged at the ox to get it started
Anxious to move on, for it was late.
But as they disappeared behind a fir tree which they skirted
Something suddenly began to agitate
The man, who shouted: 'Hey, you! Wait!'

7

'What was that you said about the water?'
Old man pauses: 'Do you want to know?'
Man replies: 'I'm not at all important
Who wins or loses interests me, though.
If you've found out, say so.

8

'Write it down. Dictate it to your boy there.
Once you've gone, who can we find out from?
There are pen and ink for your employ here
And a supper we can share; this is my home.
It's a bargain: come!'

9

Turning round, the old man looks in sorrow
At the man. Worn tunic. Got no shoes.
And his forehead just a single furrow.
Ah, no winner this he's talking to.
And he softly says: 'You too?'

10

Snubbing of politely put suggestions
Seems to be unheard of by the old.

For the old man said: 'Those who ask questions
Deserve answers'. Then the boy: 'What's more, it's turning
    cold'.
'Right. Then get my bed unrolled.'

11

Stiffly from his ox the sage dismounted.
Seven days he wrote there with his friend.
And the man brought them their meals (and all the smugglers
    were astounded
At what seemed this sudden lenient trend).
And then came the end.

12

And the boy handed over what they'd written –
Eighty-one sayings – early one day.
And they thanked the man for the alms he'd given
Went round that fir and climbed the rocky way.
Who was so polite as they?

13

But the honour should not be restricted
To the sage whose name is clearly writ.
For a wise man's wisdom needs to be extracted.
So the customs man deserves his bit.
It was he who called for it.

DRIVEN OUT WITH GOOD REASON

I grew up as the son
Of well-to-do people. My parents put
A collar round my neck and brought me up
In the habit of being waited on
And schooled me in the art of giving orders. But
When I was grown up and looked about me
I did not like the people of my own class

Nor giving orders, nor being waited on
And I left my own class and allied myself
With insignificant people.

Thus
They brought up a traitor, taught him
All their tricks, and he
Betrays them to the enemy.

Yes, I give away their secrets. I stand
Among the people and explain
Their swindles. I say in advance what will happen, for I
Have inside knowledge of their plans.
The Latin of their corrupt clergy
I translate word for word into the common speech, and there
It is seen to be humbug. The scales of their justice
I take down so as to show
The fraudulent weights. And their informers report to them
That I sit among the dispossessed when they
Are plotting rebellion.

They sent me warnings and they took away
What I had earned by my work. And when I failed to reform
They came to hunt me down; however
They found
Nothing in my house but writings which exposed
Their designs on the people. So
They made out a warrant against me
Which charged me with holding low opinions, that is
The opinions of the lowly.

Wherever I go I am branded
In the eyes of the possessors, but those without possessions
Read the charge against me and offer me
Somewhere to hide. You, they tell me
Have been driven out with
Good reason.

TO THOSE BORN LATER

I

Truly, I live in dark times!
The guileless word is folly. A smooth forehead
Suggests insensitivity. The man who laughs
Has simply not yet had
The terrible news.

What kind of times are they, when
A talk about trees is almost a crime
Because it implies silence about so many horrors?
That man there calmly crossing the street
Is already perhaps beyond the reach of his friends
Who are in need?

It is true I still earn my keep
But, believe me, that is only an accident. Nothing
I do gives me the right to eat my fill.
By chance I've been spared. (If my luck breaks, I am lost.)

They say to me: Eat and drink! Be glad you have it!
But how can I eat and drink if I snatch what I eat
From the starving, and
My glass of water belongs to one dying of thirst?
And yet I eat and drink.

I would also like to be wise.
In the old books it says what wisdom is:
To shun the strife of the world and to live out
Your brief time without fear
Also to get along without violence
To return good for evil
Not to fulfil your desires but to forget them
Is accounted wise.
All this I cannot do:
Truly, I live in dark times.

II

I came to the cities in a time of disorder
When hunger reigned there.
I came among men in a time of revolt
And I rebelled with them.
So passed my time
Which had been given to me on earth.

My food I ate between battles
To sleep I lay down among murderers
Love I practised carelessly
And nature I looked at without patience.
So passed my time
Which had been given to me on earth.

All roads led into the mire in my time.
My tongue betrayed me to the butchers.
There was little I could do. But those in power
Sat safer without me: that was my hope.
So passed my time
Which had been given to me on earth.

Our forces were slight. Our goal
Lay far in the distance
It was clearly visible, though I myself
Was unlikely to reach it.
So passed my time
Which had been given to me on earth.

III

You who will emerge from the flood
In which we have gone under
Remember
When you speak of our failings
The dark time too
Which you have escaped.

For we went, changing countries oftener than our shoes
Through the wars of the classes, despairing
When there was injustice only, and no rebellion.

And yet we know:
Hatred, even of meanness
Contorts the features.
Anger, even against injustice
Makes the voice hoarse. Oh, we
Who wanted to prepare the ground for friendliness
Could not ourselves be friendly.

But you, when the time comes at last
And man is a helper to man
Think of us
With forbearance.

MOTTO TO THE SVENDBORG POEMS

Refuged beneath this Danish thatched roof, friends
I follow your struggle. I send to you now
As from time to time in the past, my poems, frightened into
      existence
By deadly visions across Sound and foliage.
Use cautiously those that reach you.
Yellowed books, fragmentary reports
Are my sources. If we see one another again
I will gladly go back to learning with you.

MOTTO
In the dark times
Will there also be singing?
Yes, there will also be singing
About the dark times.